The LONG and the SHORT
and the TALL

THE
LONG
AND THE
SHORT
AND THE
TALL

The Story of a Marine Combat Unit in the Pacific

By ALVIN M. JOSEPHY, Jr.

INTRODUCTION BY GENERAL A. A. VANDEGRIFT

PHOTOGRAPHS BY MARINE CORPS COMBAT PHOTOGRAPHERS

ZENGER PUBLISHING CO., INC.
P.O. BOX 9883 ● WASHINGTON, D.C. 20015

Manufactured in the United States of America

Library of Congress Cataloging in Publication Data

Josephy, Alvin M   1915-
  The long and the short and the tall.

  Reprint of the 1946 ed. published by Knopf, New York.
  1. World War, 1939-1945--Regimental histories--United States--Marine Corps. 3d Division.
  2. United States. Marine Corps. 3d Division--History. 3. World War, 1939-1945--Guam.
  4. Iwo Jima, Battle of, 1945.   I. Title.
D769.37 3d.J6 1979 940.54'12'73   79-20013
ISBN 0-89201-081-9

This book was written for

ROSAMOND AND DIANE

IF THERE WAS ONE SONG that could be called *the* song of all the theaters of the war against the Axis, it was "Bless 'Em All." Almost every unit and branch of service in the European and the Pacific theaters had its own special lyrics for the catchy tune. The British claimed that they were the first to start singing it. Australians challenged the claim. On Tulagi a New Zealander told us that the song was sung in Kipling's day by Empire troops in India.

In the Pacific, Marines carried it with them to Guadalcanal and took it on to the other islands they invaded, changing the lyrics of the verse to keep up with the times. The chorus, however, remained substantially the same:

> *"Bless 'em all, bless 'em all,*
> *The long and the short and the tall,*
> *Bless all the swabbies and dogfaces too,*
> *Bless all the generals, and above all bless you!*
> *Oh, we're saying goodbye to them all,*
> *As back to our foxholes we crawl;*
> *There'll be no promotion*
> *This side of the ocean,*
> *So cheer up, Gyrenes, bless 'em all."* *

"Swabbies," of course, were sailors; "dogfaces" were G.I.s; and "Gyrenes" were G.I. Marines. To all of them who sang "Bless 'Em All" on the islands of the Pacific this book is dedicated.

* Copyright by Sam Fox Publishing Co., New York, N. Y. Printed by special permission.

ACKNOWLEDGMENT

The author wishes to thank the *Infantry Journal* for permission to reprint certain material included in Chapters VII, IX, and X.

Introduction

THIS BOOK was written by a Marine Corps combat correspondent about the experiences in the Pacific of the 3d Marine Division. In many ways those experiences were typical of what occurred to the other Marine divisions that also fought the Japanese through the islands of the South, Southwest, and Central Pacific.

These divisions—we finished the war with six of them—were in and out of action in battle after battle, commencing with Pearl Harbor. Their dead lie in cemeteries in the Solomons, the Gilberts, the Marshalls, the Carolines, the Marianas, New Britain, the Philippines, the Volcanos, the Ryukyus, and elsewhere. While the war in Europe was being pressed against the Germans, these Marines were moving from one island to another, wiping out the Japanese garrisons and creating the preconditions for setting up new American bases, ever closer to the Japanese mainland.

What the author has done in this book is to give the reader a Marine's eye-view of his outfit's role in a phase of this uninterrupted offensive. As the war progressed, Americans at home became used to such words as "divisions," "gains," "landings," "mopping-up," and "enemy counterattack." This book tells what lay behind those words—what it was like to the men in the divisions when they made new landings and gains, faced enemy counterattacks, and underwent periods of mopping-up. It also tells of other things that were related to the work of a Marine division overseas—the business of training, of traveling and making camp, and of living in some of the worst terrain and climate in the world.

The reader may wonder what a Marine combat correspondent was. He was first and foremost a Marine. He went through boot camp and learned to shoot a rifle and use a bayonet. He was an enlisted man and lived, worked, and fought with his outfit. His primary function overseas was to send back stories and recordings about the men in his outfit for use in home-town newspapers and on local radio stations. Through him people back home were often thrilled to read or hear what their boy or their neighbor's boy in the Marine Corps did. At all times overseas, however, the combat correspondent was at the disposal of his field commanding officer for assignment to any duty. In combat he landed with his outfit and, if he was needed, he fought with it. Many combat correspondents received decorations for heroism. Many were killed or wounded doing their duty under fire.

Here, then, is a division of Marines, a division which, the *Washington Post* once said, "knows everything there is to know about the Japs." Certainly, in combat, the men of the 3d Marine Division had many opportunities to meet and become acquainted with the Japanese enemy. This is the story that is told in this book.

General A. A. Vandegrift
Commandant of the Marine Corps

Foreword

IN January 1944 I received orders from Brigadier General Robert L. Denig, Director of what was then called the Division of Public Relations of the Marine Corps in Washington, to report as a combat correspondent to the 3d Marine Division somewhere in the South Pacific.

The 3d Division was under the command of Major General Allen Hal Turnage. It had gone overseas a year before, in January and February 1943, and had trained in New Zealand and Guadalcanal. On November 1, 1943, it had invaded Bougainville in the northern Solomon Islands. The campaign had been a particularly uncomfortable one, waged in one of the worst rain forests in the South Pacific. After a couple of months, a perimeter defense had been established in the jungle, behind which an American airfield was made secure, and the Division had been relieved by U. S. Army troops.

About the time the Division left Bougainville, I sailed from San Francisco to join it. I traveled on a Liberty ship as a casual —a man without a unit. It was a monotonous 24-day trip. The entire time we were on watch against Japanese submarines, airplanes, and surface raiders. We saw none and arrived safely in Noumea, New Caledonia, a Free French possession.

Noumea at that time was a large United Nations forward base. It shuttled men and supplies northward to the fronts in the Solomons and New Guinea. Hospitals on the island were filled with Marine veterans from the Cape Gloucester and the Bougainville campaigns. A large Marine casual camp formed us into units—newcomers and old-timers who had recovered from wounds and illnesses—and sent us on to the outfits in the field.

At that time—February 1944—four Marine divisions had

been in action. The 1st Division had been at Guadalcanal and Cape Gloucester, the 2d Division at Guadalcanal and Tarawa, the 3d at Bougainville, and the 4th in the Marshalls. But since the beginning of the war many of the men in those outfits had seen action in units smaller than divisions—in defense and Raider battalions and in other special commands. They had been at Pearl Harbor, Midway, Makin, Tulagi, New Georgia, and Eniwetok. They had been fighting for a long time, but there were still thousands of miles to go and many Jap-held island chains to cross before we could begin to hammer the war home on the Japanese mainland.

I found the 3d Division back in the jungle of Guadalcanal, preparing and training for another blow against the enemy. To our men who had just come out of their first battle, Bougainville, the end of the war seemed incredibly far away. The Solomons was still an advanced area. Ahead of us were Truk and the fortresses of the Carolines. Bougainville and New Guinea, despite the long, painful Allied operations on both islands, were still full of Japs. Our victories at Kwajalein and Eniwetok cheered us, but those islands seemed no closer to Japan than Guadalcanal. About all we had done, we thought, was to secure Australia and our southern supply line across the Pacific. We could visualize many more Bougainvilles, perhaps more Tarawas, in an interminable series of invasions on island after island up the long ladder that led to Tokyo.

I was assigned to the 12th Marine Regiment of the 3d Division. It was the Division's artillery regiment. Altogether, I spent approximately three months on Guadalcanal and Tulagi, which had been converted into advance bases and staging areas since the Marines had first landed there a year and a half before. During the time we waited and trained on Guadalcanal, American forces consolidated our positions in the Solomons by occupying without opposition Emirau and the Green Islands. From time to time, rumors swept through our outfit that we were about to leave on another big operation. At first we thought we might be going to Kavieng or Rabaul—large Jap bases in New Ireland and New Britain. But our strategy in the Pacific changed during those months. Our successes in the Marshall Islands made it possible to think of a move that would bypass many of the most formidable Jap bases in the South Pacific. Near the end of May we did pack our gear and load transports that had come to get us, and we knew we were finally going into action again. That is where this book starts.

During my service with the different units of the 3d Marine Division I discovered that to the Marines in the Pacific the war against the Japs broke down simply to a series of one campaign after the other, punctuated by periods of mopping-up and rest. Often there was little time to rest—merely time enough to absorb replacements and undergo training necessary to prepare for the next move. When one looks at the records of the various Marine divisions, it is seen that almost without interruption, after Guadalcanal, every existing division was just going into action or just coming out. That perhaps was the way it should have been. Men joined the Marines to fight. And the Corps itself always existed as an organization ready to move into action at short notice. When Pearl Harbor came, America had few other fighting men so well prepared to resist the enemy as the Marines were. In fact, on that "day of infamy" many of us who were civilians at the time were no doubt inspired to join the Corps by the fact that Marines were already facing the enemy at Pearl Harbor, Wake, Guam, and the Philippines. And there were Marines also on Iceland, Midway, and Samoa, ready for whatever might come.

This book, which concerns the men of the 3d Marine Division during the time I was with it, was not meant to be about myself. But, at times, the only way I have been able to tell the story of what we saw and did and went through was to tell the story from a personal viewpoint. As an enlisted Marine, sharing the life and views and feelings of the men in the ranks around me, there were times when all I could relate was what happened to me or to the unit to which I was attached.

The story, as I tell it, is not a complete history of the Division, nor is it a technical account of a military organization. It is the tale of an outfit as any sergeant might know it and tell about it from the moment he joined it until the moment he left it and only from his own little private niche in the unit. It is what somebody might write home if at the time it did not interfere with military security, or what he might like to write in a diary if keeping a diary were allowed.

One final word. As a combat correspondent, I was not a member of a rifle squad, and I did not go into combat as a regular infantryman. To all of us who were combat correspondents, living with the infantrymen, it was often a very sad experience to watch our friends go into combat and later see only some of them come back. I hope that this book will help preserve the memory of the men in our Division who died for the rest of us, and that it will also give people who have not lived with Marines an appreciation of how these men died that Japan might be beaten.

A. M. J., JR.

Contents

Illustrations

*The LONG and the SHORT
and the TALL*

I

Up the Pacific

NEAR the end of May 1944, we left Guadalcanal for good. On the morning we took off it rained, just as it had rained almost every morning we could remember having spent on the island. The bugle woke us at three in the drizzling blackness. We could hear reveille sounding in camps all through the coconut grove. By the time we were dressed there was a busy stirring along the roads that cut through the grove. Galley fires were roaring, and trucks and jeeps were ploughing through the mud and mist.

We made our packs hurriedly in the darkness, feeling tense and expectant over what lay ahead. After a hasty breakfast, we left our bedding rolls and locked seabags with the men who would make up what we called the rear echelon. These men, mostly supply and administrative personnel, would remain behind on Guadalcanal to strike our camp, then would follow us with our gear to wherever we were going and rejoin us as soon as the battle was over. Some of us envied the members of the rear echelon. Others of us looked down on them or viewed them indifferently. It was their job, and somebody had to do it. Moreover, a good many of them were combat veterans. This was just one operation they would be missing.

"I'll be on the next one," a quartermaster clerk said defensively as he watched us put on our packs and combat gear. "And don't worry. There'll *be* a next one."

We were the artillery regiment of the division, so we rode to the beach. The artillery always seemed to have lots of vehicles for moving guns, ammunition, and communications equipment. This morning the regiment's trucks were drawn up in the mud around our camp, and we felt lucky that we wouldn't have to slog several miles to the beach through the mud and rain like the infantry. Our commanding officer, a tall first lieutenant from Westwood Village, Cal., stood next to one of the trucks and made a speech.

"We're splitting up," he said. "Half this outfit is going on one ship with me. The other half will be on another ship." He named a second officer as being in charge of the other group. "When we land," he went on, "we'll be together again. I want to wish everybody luck and hope we all get through this thing without too much trouble."

The men stood in the drizzle beneath their packs and helmets and listened soberly. The Lieutenant was a serious young man. His name was Rodgers, and he had been a football player at U. C. L. A. He was going to be killed in this coming operation. So were a lot of the Marines listening to him.

When the Lieutenant was through talking we said goodbye to the fellows staying behind and piled into the trucks. A fat, easy-going radio man paused to pay ten dollars to two of the cooks who would be in the rear echelon. The cooks had killed a crocodile in one of Guadalcanal's rivers the day before. They had brought the crocodile in over the hood of their jeep and had cut off the head and boiled it in a can of hot water to loosen the teeth. The radio man was paying for a necklace to be made of the croc's teeth.

"I'll give you the rest when you deliver the necklace to me," he said to the cooks. "And don't figure on my getting bumped off. I'm going to stay specially alive to get this ten dollars back if you don't deliver."

There were no bands, no bugle calls, no whistles to sound us off. The men who were staying behind gathered in the mud and watched us sleepily as the drivers started the trucks' engines.

"If you have any trouble, just send for us," a clerk in the personnel section called.

"What will you feather merchants do?" someone yelled back from one of the trucks. "Come to the rescue with your damned old typewriters?"

"The pen is mightier than the sword," the clerk answered. He dug his hands in his pockets and looked at us sadly.

Slowly the trucks ground into gear and lurched off. We bumped through the grove, and it was light enough for us to get a last look at what had been our home for many months. Though the grove was one of the more bearable spots on Guadalcanal, it was still a humid mudhole. Before the war it had been a coconut plantation. The trees stood in straight rows—many square miles of them. It was far from where the fighting on the island had been and, except for a few splintered trees where lone Jap bombs had fallen, there were no marks of war. When our Division had moved into the site after the Bougainville campaign in January 1944, the men had cleared off the grass and brush beneath the coconut trees, but this attempt to create a neat, orderly camp had resulted mainly in exposing the earth to the rain and thus creating mud. Originally, when the threat from Jap bombers had still existed, we had dug foxholes beside our tents. But soon after the turn of the year our campaign in Bougainville had borne fruit, and Jap planes that had been raiding Guadalcanal disappeared from the skies.

We gazed at the different camps beneath the trees as we bounced by and wished the whole area back to the natives.

"I wonder who's going to get this place after the war?" one of the men in our truck asked.

"Give it to the Japs," a corporal exclaimed. "As part of their punishment."

"I'd hate to have to do garrison duty on this rock," a third man said. "I pity whoever's stationed here."

"You won't know this place," a sergeant said quietly. "It will all be fixed up nicely for tourists. They'll have hotels here and bus lines running around, with men with megaphones pointing out the sites." He waved toward the grove. " 'Here's where the 3d Marine Division had its liberty after the Bougainville campaign,' " he mimicked.

"Some liberty!" a man muttered.

Actually we had several times seriously discussed who would get Guadalcanal after the war. The coconut groves, we understood, belonged to the English soap concern of Lever Brothers, and no doubt it would get them back. From our point of view, it didn't much matter who held the island as long as it was in friendly hands and we personally didn't have to do garrison duty there. For peacetime nothing much nearer to hell on earth could be imagined. The memories of Guadalcanal that we were taking away with us, and that we were sure would stay with us all our lives, were of rain and mud, mosquitoes and heat, fungus and rot and loneliness, physical discomfort and mental boredom. *That* was "the Canal."

It didn't occur to us that we might find the same things where we were going, or that we might find them everywhere we went as long as the war lasted. When the men had been fighting at Bougainville, Guadalcanal had seemed like a paradise. But for more than two months on Bougainville our men had endured the heights—or depths—of misery: inches of muddy water in the foxholes, tangled, almost impenetrable jungle, cold rations, and no cover against the ceaseless rain. Back on the Canal, however, they recalled the tents and cots, the hot chow, the makeshift showers, sunlight, an occasional cool breeze. It was, as a first sergeant had said, a matter of relativity. "Oh, to get back to Guadalcanal!" Then, after the first effects of the new improvements wore off: "Oh, to get somewhere else!" Now we were going somewhere else.

We kissed Guadalcanal goodbye. We never wanted to see it again. But, once more, we might be going from bad to worse. We didn't know.

None of us knew certainly what our next destination would be. There were lots of rumors and many arguments. The consensus among the men was Truk. Those of us who believed we were going to Truk were awed by the thought. Not a few of us were pretty scared. For Truk was supposed to be the Jap Pearl Harbor. It lay in the center of the enemy strongholds in the Caroline chain, directly north of the Solomons. For a year we had been moving up the ladder towards it. New Georgia—Kolombangara—Vella Lavella—Bougainville —the Green Islands. Now we were like an arrow pointing at Truk. And, lately, our warships and airplanes had been shelling and bombing Truk and other Caroline islands, which sounded to us like a softening-up process. The short-wave radio from San Francisco had been hinting at something. "The Japs are expecting a possible invasion of Truk by American forces," the announcer said. American forces. That was us, and it didn't sound good.

All the way down to the beach from the coconut grove we could see long columns of our infantry winding across the meadows and through the tall yellow grass that stretched toward the hills and fringes of jungle. Occasionally we passed a unit wading through the mud at the side of the road. They looked up at us with tired, envious eyes and took without comment, the mud-splashing our vehicles gave them. Near the beach a machine-gun section from one of the infantry regiments swore at the vehicles ahead of us. Some mud had splattered over the men's cleaned, greased weapons. They put the machine-gun parts down on the grass to examine the damage. A Pfc looked up at us cockily as we went by.

"B.T.O.s [big-time operators], aren't you?" he shouted.

Our men laughed. "Are you jealous?" one of the fellows in our truck taunted.

We passed the machine-gun section and drove along a sandy road that paralleled the beach. It had stopped raining, but the sky was still gray. The area was packed with Marines, waiting in groups and units, or lounging off the road, back from the shore. On the sand were big placards listing the names of the ships standing off that part of the beach. Men going on those ships waited along the road and back in the jungle for landing boats to come in and get them.

As we crept along the road, through the milling troops, we looked out at the channel at the convoy on which we were going to sail. It looked very big to us—bigger than any convoy our men had ever seen in the Pacific.

"The European war must be slackening up," one of our veterans said. "They never give us that many ships before."

"They been doing some building back home," another man said. "Besides, this is a big operation."

For a brief instant the reference to the operation made our stomachs sink. It was better not to refer ominously to what lay ahead—better either not to discuss it at all, or else talk it out fully like a business deal. But no sidewise references.

We looked for ships that we knew. Each one of us had been on transports before, some of us on many. The ships were like members of a large family. Some were old-timers that had been plying back and forth among the islands since before Guadalcanal. Others were newcomers, taking part in their first amphibious operation. There were fat, blue-gray transports, hung with life rafts; green LSTs and LCIs; little destroyer escorts; patrol craft. Across the channel near the dull gray outline of Tulagi lay two flat-tops—rare and exciting to see in the Pacific. In the earlier campaigns Marines never saw them. Either there were too few of them or they were always out of sight, over the horizon, guarding against interference to the convoy from Jap ships and planes. The sight of two of them now made our hearts skip. We were really getting some power for this push.

One of our men pointed out the "Unholy Four"—four old

veteran transports that had participated in every amphibious landing since the invasion of Guadalcanal.

"I came up on one of them to Guadalcanal," the veteran said. He had been with a Raider battalion at the time, had been wounded, had gone to a hospital in the United States, and was now overseas again, this time with the 3d Division. "Maybe I can get on the same ship," he said. "It'd be okay. The old crew's probably still on her. Good bunch!"

Among the "Unholy Four" I recognized one of the transports that had brought me up from New Caledonia to Guadalcanal to join the 3d Division three months before. I hoped that I would be assigned to her once more, if only to see again the sailors I had known at that time. It was a comforting thought that I might go into battle aboard a ship I knew and with men who would remember me.

When our truck pulled up, however, it was opposite a placard with the names of four other ships. One of them was the *Crescent City*, an old-timer.

"That's your ship," the driver said as we climbed off the truck.

A gunnery sergeant stared out at the transport. "She's all right," he said thoughtfully. "I been on her. She's clean and modern. Good holds."

The driver parked the truck and walked with us into a clearing that Seabees had made on the side of the road away from the beach. We took off our packs and helmets and sat down among the fallen coconut trees. Some of the men took out paper-covered books and magazines. Others produced packs of cards from their helmets and started games of pinochle and poker. Some just sat silently, watching the others or nodding on their knees trying to doze.

"I will be there with the forty-fifth wave," our truck driver said to us laughingly, as he stretched out among the rubble of coconuts and tree fronds. He was a stout, heavy-set man of Russian ancestry, about thirty-five, with a flabby face and a good-natured grin. When he laughed, his whole face seemed to shake. A platoon sergeant, he had been in the Corps for almost twenty years. He was not really a driver; he was the noncom in charge of our unit's transportation. He was staying behind to help close up the motor-transport section and bring up the vehicles, personnel, and equipment not needed during the fighting. He had driven one of the trucks to the beach himself because he was shorthanded. Also, he wanted to see us off.

"It is going to be murder for you poor fellows," he kidded us in a voice that still had a slight accent to it. "You know, they are counting on sixty-percent casualties. I will be there in time to bury a lot of you."

"How come you thirty-year men always get out of combat?" one of the Marines asked without smiling. "You're always making cracks about us reserves, but every time there's a fight, who's holding down soft spots in the rear echelon? You regulars!"

The Russian laughed and rubbed his face. "We are smart," he said. "We know how to take care of ourselves."

We had a long wait at the beach. Lieutenant Rodgers and the noncoms in charge of our unit stood at the water's edge, waiting for boarding instructions. Landing boats roared in all morning from the transports. Beachmasters and Navy and Seabee officers in charge of the loading hustled individual units aboard, supervised the manhandling of rations and small-arms ammunition that units carried with them, and ordered the small boats out again as quickly as they had come in.

Among the fallen coconut trees, we dozed and read and swatted mosquitoes and flies. The excitement and tension of the early part of the morning wore off.

"Rush, rush, rush, then wait," one man grumbled.

A few members of a surveying unit traded old torn magazines from home.

"Look at this," one of the Marines exclaimed.

He had a copy of *Life* opened to a series of pictures of people back home having a good time in Miami. A group of men crowded around him and gazed at the pictures. No one said anything. Finally a little fellow with a baby face and fuzz where he should have had a mustache said, "Ah, they don't know there's a war going on."

A private with a carbine and two knives on his cartridge belt looked at the little fellow disgustedly. "What do you want them to do?" he said. "Wear black mourning and go around beating their chests? If you were home, that's what you'd be doing too."

The man with the magazine pulled away and continued thumbing through it. The private with the carbine and two knives lay down among the dry, cracking coconut fronds and put his helmet under his head.

"There's no equal sacrifice in this war anyway," he said. "Some people aren't ever going to know what went on. The sooner you realize that, the better off you are."

A long, bony man who had been sitting on a log, reading a comic book, looked up and nodded.

"You ain't just a-kidding," he said. "I got a letter from a guy was sent home after Bougainville with a bad leg. You know what he wrote? People says, what outfit were you in? He says, the 3d Division. They say, where you been? He says, Bougainville. They say, where's that, in North Carolina? How do you like that?"

"When I go home," said the little fellow with the baby face, "I'm just going to tell people that I was on Guadalcanal. Everybody's heard of Guadalcanal. And they feel sorry for you if they know you were there."

A little before noon a line of landing boats hurtled onto the beach, and Lieutenant Rodgers called the outfit into column. We streamed aboard the LCVPs. The Navy coxswains of the little boats regarded us with interest.

"Any guy here from Texas?" one of them called.

A corporal turned around and pushed his helmet back on his head. "I'm from Lubbock," he said in a loud voice.

The coxswain grinned. "You can swim out, mate," he laughed.

We all laughed, a mild sort of laugh, like the laughs in which we had been indulging all morning. Time was passing. We were going from one phase to another—from camp to the beach to the transport. There was no going back. We were taking steps that led only to one place. But we were doing it lightheartedly. It was fine.

We manhandled some artillery ammunition boxes and some map cases and surveying gear into the boat with us. Then the coxswains raised the ramp. They were two young-looking sailors—like all the coxswains manning LCVPs. They didn't seem eighteen. They were like kids just entering high school —the kind of young roughnecks who like to wrestle and speed and live excitingly. Handling LCVPs seemed to be the right kind of job for them. They could race the powerful motors and speed the little ships through the surf, sending them in circles through clusters of other boats and just narrowly miss anyone who came within calling distance. They got great fun out of scaring the Marine passengers—aiming straight at another landing boat, then veering suddenly away from it at top speed to miss a collision by a fraction of an inch. They liked to hear the Marines scream and curse. They threw their heads back and laughed as if it were great sport. At least, that was the way it seemed to us passengers.

We raced other LCVPs out to our transport. The race was another diversion for our thoughts. When we clambered aboard the transport, hand over hand, up the swaying cargo net, we hurried for decent beds, or sacks, as we called them. We were wise to the little things that meant the difference between misery and mere discomfort aboard a transport, and we felt fortunate that we were among the first men to be brought out to our ship. It meant we had first choice, at least, in the selection of sacks. While the officers went to state-rooms in the superstructure, we hurried forward on the main deck to openings that led down to the holds. The first men

OUR COCONUT GROVE CAMP ON GUADALCANAL. Four of our men wade up the company street after a heavy rain.

AMPHIBIOUS TRACTORS AT GUAM. All around us, as we headed in on D-day, we could see low-lying amphtracs crowded with Marines.

in line had to clamber down only one deck. Members of the ship's crew, including a few hospital corpsmen, were already sleeping on that deck, but there were some empty sacks along the bulkheads. The first Marines down made a grab for the vacant berths. The other men had to continue down the ladder to the second deck—to what we called the Black Hole of Calcutta.

On the first deck I recognized a hospital corpsman whom I had met at Guadalcanal's big Navy hospital. He had been in the pharmacy there. He had a handle-bar mustache and came from New Jersey where he had owned his own pharmacy in civilian life. He recognized me the moment I entered the hold and motioned wildly to a sack near his.

"Here, quick, take it!" he roared, as Marines streamed in behind me.

I threw my gear on the rectangular piece of canvas. Later the pharmacist made me more comfortable by getting me a mattress from the bunk of a sailor who was in the sick-bay.

"What are you doing here?" I asked him after I had settled down.

"I got sick of the Canal," he said. "I got a transfer." He twisted the ends of his mustache. "Where are we going?"

I shrugged.

"Did you hear the Tokyo radio last night?"

"No," I said.

"Tokyo Annie gave the scoop. Said the 3d Marine Division was leaving Guadalcanal. Said the Japs would be waiting for you."

The anecdote was old. Every time a unit left any place on an operation, somebody bobbed up with the story that the Tokyo radio had announced all the details.

"Where did she say we were going?" I asked.

"Guam."

"Clear around the Carolines?"

"Yop."

It was a good guess, but more likely it owed its origin to

scuttlebutt circulating among the ships. We were going to flank the Carolines, the rumors went. The taking of the Marshall Islands in the Central Pacific would allow us now to change our strategy. We would hop over some islands. Truk would be by-passed.

"We have a lot of Guamanian sailors aboard," the pharmacist said. "They've been gathered from all over the fleet. We're going to take them home."

I went up on deck to see how widely the scuttlebutt had traveled and just how many men with influence were giving it credence. A driver for a colonel, for instance, might smile knowingly when you asked him about Guam point blank—which would be pretty good proof.

The decks were swarming with Marines. Some were still climbing up the cargo net, reaching the deck red-faced and puffing, and then bolting for a hold, in the hope of still being able to get a good sack. Suddenly I bumped into a chief yeoman I had met on the transport coming up from New Caledonia.

"Well," he said, as he recognized me, "last time I saw you we left you on this island."

"What are you doing on this ship?" I asked. He had been with the staff of the commander of a group of transports when I had come up from New Caledonia.

"We transferred the flag over to this ship," he said. "The whole staff came over."

That meant that I would have a lot of friends on this ship —men I had met on the other vessel. It was good news.

"This is a good ship for you Marines," he said. "There's ice water for drinking and fresh water for washing all day long—if you don't use too much."

This was the best news yet. On the average ship the most we could expect was fresh water a couple of hours a day. Sometimes all we got with which to wash was sticky, uncomfortable, nonlathering salt water.

"Where are we going?" I asked.

He opened his mouth and laughed loudly. "I don't know," he answered. "Nobody tells me anything. But," he looked around and came closer, "I'll tell you what the scuttlebutt is. It's Wake Island."

I abandoned further attempts to try to find out our destination.

Just before we left, some final mail was brought aboard and distributed to us. Most of it was second-class stuff—packages that had been three months and more coming from the States. Postal clerks on Guadalcanal had made a frantic last-minute effort to sort the heavy mail so that we would have it before we departed.

In our hold there were some funny gifts. A youth from one of the Dakotas opened a big box and pulled out a feather pillow.

"My golly!" he exclaimed, scratching his head. "When I was on Bougainville I wrote my mother and told her how much I missed a good soft pillow. Now look, she sends me one!"

It was a good gift for the transport, but nothing to carry ashore on D-day. The youth made use of it while we were aboard, then presented it to one of the sailors before we went over the side into battle.

Another man got a kewpie doll in that mail, and still another a pair of silk pajamas. There was also lots of food. A fat, roly-poly communications man from Texas got a cardboard container full of cans of Spam. He grunted disgustedly and heaved the whole package overboard. There were also letters. The mail was handed out by a gunnery sergeant sitting on one of the top sacks in the hold. He called out the men's names and sailed the letters in the direction of those answering. Then the men moved off by themselves, opened the letters carefully and read them slowly, again and again. They dwelt on each detail, whether serious or trivial, as though planning to hoard it among the memories they would carry ashore into combat. In the days that followed, as we sailed to where we were going, those letters were pulled out again and again and read and quoted. They were important, both for what they said and for what they were. Later some of them, carried in pants pockets, in helmet liners, in packs, were to be soaked with blood.

We set sail early one afternoon. A Navy chief, who had been on the ship that had brought me up from New Caledonia, was in charge of the signal bridge on the *Crescent City*, and he let me come up where the breeze blew fresh and cool and where I could see around me the full panorama of our convoy. We were more than a division of Marines. Another convoy, sailing over the horizon from us, carried what was known as the 1st Provisional Marine Brigade, made up of the 4th and 22d Marine Regiments, and the members of the III Amphibious Corps, under the command of Marine Major General Roy S. Geiger. General Geiger was in overall command of our assault. We—the 3d Division—would make one beachhead, and the Brigade would make the other; then we would link. The 3d Division was led by Major General Turnage, who had commanded our men at Bougainville. The Brigade was commanded by Major General Lemuel C. Shepherd. The two regiments of the Brigade had each been in previous actions. The 4th was made up of old Raiders, veterans of Makin, Guadalcanal, New Georgia, and Bougainville. The 22d was the outfit that had taken Eniwetok in the Marshall Islands a few months before. They were two good outfits, rugged and experienced.

Our own Division, we liked to think, was a crack outfit. We had three infantry regiments—the 3d, 9th, and 21st Marines; the artillery regiment, the 12th, to which I was attached; an engineer regiment, the 19th, made up of engineers, pioneers, and Seabees; and the usual division troops, including tanks, amphibious tractors, war dogs, MPs, signal units, and so forth. A good part of the infantry were on LSTs, proceeding ahead of us. The LSTs were slower than the transports, so we gave them a head start. From the men's point of view it was not desirable to travel on LSTs. There was less fresh water and less storage space for fresh food, and after a few days the diet usually got down to C rations and canned luncheon meat. But the assault troops would be landed, where we were going, on amphibious tractors which would take them over a reef, and the tractors could be launched into the water easily from the ramps of the LSTs. So the troops of the first waves were put on the LSTs to ride out on the tractors on D-day morning.

The rest of the infantry were on the transports around us. There were three long columns of ships in our group, guarded by a ring of small destroyer escorts and patrol craft. Far away we could see the silhouette of a carrier or a cruiser, and we knew that, somewhere out of sight from us, other elements of our fleet were screening us from possible trouble. We rode along peacefully through the sparkling sea, with scarcely a thought for submarines or enemy planes, perferring, unconsciously perhaps, to leave such worries to the Navy—our hosts on the transport.

It became hotter as we moved up the Pacific, and soon it was announced to us over the ship's loud-speaker that we had crossed the Equator. The event was exciting to some of our men.

"First time north of the Equator in twenty-three months," a private exclaimed. "It damn well makes you feel different. Like a new man."

"Smell that breeze," said another man. "It's fresher."

It became unbearably hot in the dark holds, even on the first deck down, and most of us slept topside. We would stretch a poncho on the hard deck, under one of the landing boats if we could find room, and gaze at the sky and try to locate the North Star. It was important to us that we were again in the hemisphere where we could see the North Star, after having been for so long beneath the Southern Cross. Perhaps it was because the North Star seemed to be something that linked us with home—home, so far away and so long ago. Polaris was part of a sky that was familiar in our life back there, and coming on it again was almost like moving in the direction of the States.

One day we put into one of the big lagoons of the Marshall Islands. It was a staging area. There were hundreds of ships all around us. We took on fuel and supplies, and our officers visited each other on the different transports for last-minute conferences. We were told we could get off letters saying that we were going into action. We wrote quickly and casually— the usual thing about not worrying, everything was fine but don't expect to hear from me for a while, etc. We gave our letters to our unit postal clerks who took them ashore for mailing at a Navy post office on one of the atolls.

One man, a sergeant in charge of a machine-gun crew, talked of his wife and son back in Beverly Hills. His name was Dale DeWitt, and he had been wounded at Bougainville. There seemed to be a lot he wanted to say, both to and about his family, but words were hard and thoughts were confused.

"Combat's a damned funny thing," he said. "It creeps up on you as though it were going to be another passing day in your life. You feel it getting closer and closer, but you don't pay any extra attention to it. You don't do anything to prepare for the worst, you don't tie up the strings in your life or anything. You just naturally assume that everything will take care of itself."

A lot of us felt like that—not scared yet, not dramatic, not even excited. On the surface we were calm and matter-of-fact. Our stomachs were comfortable, even if a bit uneasy with the vaguely sinking feeling that some people get when they are called on to address large gatherings. Where we were uncomfortable was in our minds, because there we were confused—and we didn't know what we were confused about. It had something to do with home and family and possible extinction without leaving a trace, no doubt caused by our realization that we were moving close to death and had no philosophy with which to face it. A few of the men had a deep

religious faith, and a handful had some sort of settled philosophy. But it would not be true to say that all the men in
either of these groups were prepared to face what lay ahead
of us.

One night while we were lying in the lagoon word came
over our ship's loud-speakers that the Allies had landed in
France to open the second front. The news was electrifying.
The men went out on deck and whooped and cheered and
clapped each other on the back. Some of us had brothers or
cousins in the "show" halfway round the world. We boasted
about them, sure that they had been in the first wave.

"Now you watch," one of the men said. "They'll finish up
with old Mr. Hitler toot sweet and be over here to help us,
and then this thing will be over before you know it."

The oneness of the war had never before seemed so clear to
us. Now it was dramatically vivid what beating the Nazis
was going to mean to us in the Pacific. It also made us think,
for a moment at least, of the price the men in Europe might
be paying.

"God," one man remarked, "what casualties those poor
guys must be having!"

The point was food for thought, for casualties were sacrifice. We knew that. We had always known that a man dead
in battle has died in an effort to make something else possible.
But we had rarely given thought to what that "something
else" was. Now we could see it graphically: the men dying on
the Normandy beaches were dying so that other men could
get a foothold there and press inward and reach Germany and
vanquish the Nazis. Then they—the ones who survived—could
come over to the Pacific and help us, and in time all of us
would get home. Perhaps this was a selfish way of looking at
it, but it was realistic.

One evening soon afterwards we pulled up anchor and
sailed out of the big lagoon. Our convoy pointed west. The

next morning meetings were called in the holds. Our unit commanders came down the ladders with relief maps and aerial photographs, and we gathered around them in little knots to be briefed.

"On June 15," Lieutenant Rodgers announced to our group, "the 2d and 4th Marine Divisions are going to hit Saipan in the Marianas Islands. We will stand by as floating reserve. If they don't need us, we are going to invade Guam."

This confirmation of the rumor that we might be going to Guam excited many of the men. Guam would be the first inhabited American possession that we would retake from the Japs. It had been seized by the Japanese in their first rush southward in December 1941, after Pearl Harbor. Our small detachment of Marines and sailors stationed there had not had a chance. With the exception of one man, they had all been either killed or taken prisoner.

Lieutenant Rodgers showed us where we would land, what we would find, and what we would have to do. He showed us where the other division units would land and where the Marine Brigade would establish its beachhead and then link up with us.

"There'll be an Army division too," he said. "Elements of the 77th will be available if we need support."

When the briefing was over, we went back on deck to talk it over. It seemed as if we were streaking through the water now, trying to get to the Marianas as fast as we could. These were dangerous waters to be sailing through. We were in the heart of an ocean area long ruled by Japan. Behind us to the east was Wake Island, up north was Marcus Island, ahead of us were the Marianas, and south of us Truk and the other Carolines—all of them still important Japanese bases.

"I wish we were taking Wake Island," one of the fellows said, as we watched the water from the rail.

"What's the matter with Guam?" a sergeant retorted. "There's civilization on Guam. A big city. I was there before

REACHING THE BEACH. It looks peaceful, but it isn't. Jap fire is coming down at these men from the Guam hills.

BEACHHEAD SECURED. Old Glory flies again on Guamanian soil. This is the CP of one of our units pushing inland.

the war when I was doing sea duty. We put in for a week. Good-looking people there."

That, of course, was important. Guam had civilization—people, houses, stores, women—which meant a lot to men who had been in the jungle a year. A captain on deck overheard our conversation.

"The capital city on Guam is pretty big," he said. "It's called Agana. Used to be a good liberty town."

On June 15 we waited anxiously for word about the landings on Saipan. The transport's chaplain made periodic reports of the battle over the ship's loud-speakers. The news he gave us was good, and it kept on being good. We got no word of the heavy casualties the men were suffering on Saipan, but we heard of progress fair enough to make it look as though we wouldn't be needed there. Nevertheless we continued to hover somewhere near the Marianas, though out of sight of land.

Then, one day, when all of us began to think that momentarily we would start for Guam, we turned around and began racing back in the direction from which we had come. The chaplain got on the public-address system and said:

"Some poet once proclaimed that East is East and West is West and never the twain shall meet. But alas, men, they are meeting now. We are returning to the Marshall Islands."

We didn't think the announcement was funny. We didn't understand it. We felt let down. We had been on edge for a fight. Now something funny was happening and it wasn't a fight. The short-wave radio from San Francisco that night hinted at what was happening, and several of us listened to it in the chiefs' wardroom: The Japanese fleet was coming out to fight; enemy units had been spotted steaming towards the Marianas from the Philippines.

"We're running from the Jap fleet!" the chief yeoman exclaimed.

"Well, what do you want us to do? Hang around and fight

it?" another chief retorted. "Our fleet will take care of the Japs."

We put in at another big atoll in the Marshall Islands and waited. We were restless and unhappy. To make it worse, after a few days someone thoughtfully arranged for our first-class mail to be routed to our ships, and letters were distributed. What made it bad was that our folks had received our original letters saying we were going into combat. Then the landings on Saipan had been announced, and they naturally assumed that that was where we now were.

"They mention the 2d and 4th Divisions, but not the 3d," a father had written irritably to his son. "I don't know why your division never gets credit for what it does."

A lot of our people were worrying, but there was nothing we could do about it. We couldn't write now and set them straight.

To pass the time profitably we went ashore each day for exercises and swimming. From the ships the little islands of the atoll looked like sparkling gems—neat little movie sets of glistening white sand, liquid green lagoons, and graceful coconut trees. The sky looked beautifully blue and the ocean breakers so white that surely, we thought, man could wish for no more attractive setting. But, as everywhere in the South Seas, the beauty always hid something unattractive. On some islands it was disease. On others it was unbearable heat. In the Marshalls the beautiful white sand turned out to be sharp coral that burned and cut our feet, and the cool, green water of the lagoons sheltered fungus that infected our ears and parts of our bodies.

The little LCVPs of our transports took us ashore in units each day. We got out on the reefs and waded ashore and then marched around the atolls over the jagged, burning coral, or tramped across the islands through sharp-edged grass that nicked and scratched. It wasn't pleasant. The unhappiest part of it was that we wore out our shoes on the coral; and on our ship, at least, there were no extra shoes to distribute to the men. We walked around all day in wet shoes, and gradually they wore so thin that in wading ashore we could feel the coral cutting into our soles.

We also had a clothes problem. We had originally thought that we would need only enough clothes to see us through the short transport trip and a few days of combat, and that soon after we had secured our beachhead new clothes would be landed and distributed to us. Now the few shirts and pants that we had been able to cram into our combat packs were giving out, what with the dirt in our holds and the lack of laundry facilities. When we had been moving we had solved the laundry problem by tying our clothes to a long line and throwing them overboard to drag through the salt water. Sometimes the process tore the clothes, but at least the water cleaned them. Now we weren't even able to launder our khaki and dungarees that way, and we were beginning to look like a ragamuffin army.

The story was told that on one ship a well-known Marine gunner named "Slug" Marvin, an old-timer in the Corps who was already a subject of countless legends, had been the only man in our whole Division to get clean clothes for his unit. Marvin was in command of a flame-throwing and demolitions crew going in with the 21st Marines. When his men began to take on the appearance of old-clothes men, "Slug" angrily demanded clean dungarees for them. A supply sergeant turned him down. "Slug," who spoke naturally in a high screaming voice and was not in the habit of being turned down, threw a fit and threatened to lead his men ashore into combat wearing their skivvy drawers; he meant it, too. Somehow, enough extra sets of dungarees were produced. When the battle came, Marvin's team was about the only group of men to go ashore in new clothes.

We stayed in the Marshalls for several weeks, feeling like a lost and forgotten division. At length we heard that our fleet had scored a naval victory over the Jap fleet in the Philippine Sea and chased it away. But we still didn't move. Our ships took on more food and fuel, and we began to wonder how long it would be before someone decided to call off the whole expedition and send us back to Guadalcanal.

Then one day men began arriving from Saipan. The wounded had previously been going past us in hospital ships, and scuttlebutt had already told us that casualties there had been heavy. The new arrivals, newspapermen and Army and Marine officers, confirmed that rumor. They added that they had come to join us for "the new operation," so we knew that Guam was still on. They brought details of the Jap fortifications in the Marianas and stories of what kind of fight we might expect from the Japs garrisoned there. There were supposed to be about 30,000 Japs on Guam. They would have many big-gun emplacements and cave and pillbox fortifications. We were told not to expect too much from our preliminary naval and aerial bombardment, which had just gotten under way. Our shells and bombs would do a lot of damage, but Saipan had shown—as had Tarawa before it—that somehow too many Japs could live through everything we could pour onto the island. The enemy would be in caves back in the hills and in many well-hidden emplacements which our big stuff would be unable to find with direct hits.

Among the new arrivals were two Marine combat correspondents who had been sent from the States by plane a few weeks before to join us for the operation. The officers who had handled their transportation had assumed that they would find us at Saipan, and had sent them there. The men had landed in the middle of the battle, in one of the first of our transport planes to come down on Saipan. After a few days, they found out where the 3d Division really was and flew back to meet us in the Marshalls. They were like old veterans. Even though they had been out of the States only a few weeks, they had already been through a battle.

Early in the third week of July activity suddenly increased on our transports. There were more conferences of officers. New aerial photos of Guam were distributed and studied.

Preparations for sea were carried out on the decks. The landing boats were again hoisted into place and overhauled.

Then, one afternoon, we sailed.

Again the tenseness returned. Rations and machine-gun ammunition were put in the landing boats. Weapons were cleaned and thoroughly inspected. Gas masks were distributed. More briefings were held. D-day was announced: three days from that day. H-hour was named, and passwords were explained. We looked over our gear—our clothing and weapons—to be sure that everything was in order. One of the doctors passed among us, giving us informal talks on the disease and sanitation problems we would meet. We joked about the dysentery we would be sure to get, no matter what precautions we would take. We wrote final letters to leave with sailors to mail for us, and we made our last plans for what we would do when we hit the beach.

My job, about which I had been thinking for a long time, was going to be to make an eyewitness recording of the landing operation and the fighting on shore which woud be sent back for radio stations in the United States to broadcast. If my unit was caught in any tight spot, I should naturally have to fight with it. I should always be obliged to defend myself and take care of my own safety. If Lieutenant Rodgers ever needed me, I was trained to handle enough weapons to be able to fill in and be useful. But as a combat correspondent my primary mission was to help make the war more real to those at home by describing what a landing on a Jap-held island looked, felt, and sounded like.

The description of an invasion had never been made by a man participating in it. The idea was not to stay on a ship and describe it through binoculars, but to go along, talking the whole way, from the moment we went over the side until we hit the beach with an assault wave. To do this, I had a new portable film recording machine about the size and weight of a heavy suitcase. It was powered by a heavy 12-volt storage battery and a heavy converter. It was too much of a load to carry, so I had arranged to put it on a jeep and go in with the jeep. Just before we left the Marshalls I realized that the jeep would probably not be unloaded from the transport until D plus one, too late for the combat description I wanted to make. No other jeeps on our ship would go in any earlier, so I had to look for another vehicle.

In our hold were two halftracks, mounting 75mm. cannons. They belonged to the Weapons Company of the 3d Marines (one of our infantry regiments) and were under the command of a 27-year-old artillery expert, Major Laurence Gammon. They were going in with the first wave off our ship, as support for the assault troops of the 3d Regiment. I asked and received permission to transfer temporarily from the artillery outfit of the 12th Marines to Major Gammon's command for the landing and moved my equipment into one of the halftracks. I was helped by a Seabee, Electrician's Mate Second Class John Wheaton, who had volunteered to land with me as a technician, running the recording machine while I talked into a hand microphone. Wheaton had serviced moving-picture projectors for the Division on Guadalcanal and had originally been assigned to the rear echelon. Although he had a son serving in the Navy and was well on in years, he asked to come along, and I was glad to have his assistance.

The night before D-day the men in our hold sat around singing and giving their weapons a final cleaning. Some were members of my old artillery unit; others belonged to the half-track unit. DeWitt's machine-gun crew belonged to the latter outfit. His halftrack would come in with the wave behind ours.

We were not allowed to sleep topside that night, and it was hot in the hold. A tall, thin boy in the sack next to me rolled around and talked about his wife and two children in Chicago, and of how he hoped that this would be the last invasion he'd ever have to make. He was in the artillery unit, and it did turn out to be his last invasion: he was killed early in the campaign. Another boy, who had recently gotten a letter from his sister telling him that his girl friend had married someone else, whispered on and on to another man, trying to decide why girls behave as they do and whether you can trust any of them. That boy was killed, too.

Reveille was at two-thirty in the morning. It came through the loud-speaker in the hold, like a hammer hitting us on the head.

"Reveille, Reveille! All up! All up!"

Most of the sailors were already up, standing general quarters at their gun watches out on the black, silent decks. The "head" was crowded with Marines, many of whom had been there all night, smoking and talking about the landing. The little red lights around the toilets had been the only illumination in our hold, and the "head" was the natural gathering place. The room was filled with smoke and the heavy odor of sweat.

One man came back from the mess hall. "Beans and joe for breakfast," he announced.

We were disappointed. We had expected our last meal to be an unforgettable one—steak and fresh eggs perhaps.

"A swabbie said the skipper of this ship always serves beans and coffee as the last meal before a landing," the Marine who had been in the mess hall continued. "A tradition with him."

"That's all right," a man answered bitterly. "If they didn't say it was a tradition, they'd probably hand you the line that beans are filling. They stick to your ribs."

The pharmacist with the big handlebar mustache came into the head excitedly. "You want to see something?" he said. "Go up on deck."

We went up the ladder into the cold blowing night air.

Off on the horizon we saw it—a great fireworks display of red, yellow, and white lights zipping through the air, crashing out in the blackness, hovering in the sky like flares. When we listened we could hear it—a dull steady rumble like distant thunder.

A sailor at the rail nodded solemnly. "There's the Fleet,"

he said. "Been at it sixteen days. They're putting on the finishing touches."

We stared into the darkness at the far-away colored streaks. Suddenly we saw a great burst of red flame.

"See that?" said the sailor. "That's Guam."

II

"Another Little Island"

THIS was my first combat. I had never been under fire before and had a vague dread of what it would be like and how I would stand up to it. For weeks I had given my imagination full play, trying to visualize the scene on D-day as we landed on a Jap-held island and moved inland against the enemy. I tried to imagine myself wading across a reef with enemy fire coming at me. I tried to realize what it would be like when I saw my first dead American. I wanted to be prepared. I didn't want to be shocked. I thought that by such mental preparation I might take the actual event easier, and I think it did help. As the real thing approached, it seemed as if I were seeing a scene already familiar and undergoing things for which I had thoroughly rehearsed. The sounds of shells and bullets would not be strange. I had reconstructed what they would sound like from many elements in my past experience—newsreel sounds, maneuvers, etc.—and on D-day morning that was just the way they were. It was as if I had been through shellings many times, and there was nothing strange or unusual about what was going to unfold.

Back on Guadalcanal I had been in a tent with five veterans of Bougainville, men who had been overseas for sixteen to twenty-five months and who had already experienced the terrors of combat. We used to lie awake nights under our mosquito netting, listening to the pounding of the rain on our tent, and I would ask them what it had been like on Bougainville. Mostly they remembered the landing and Jap planes. Some of the waves had had to land in the face of Jap fire and had been strafed by low-flying enemy planes along the beach.

"Getting onto the beach is the worst part," one of them said. "It's a nightmare. After you're on the beach, you can try to find cover. But on the way there, you're wide open."

They also remembered the jungle and the mud and the long nights in watery foxholes, and one of the boys recalled a Jap bomb—a 500-pound aerial—that had fallen in the middle of his camp around midnight.

"It was terrible," he said. "Nobody knew what happened. You couldn't see. There was somebody moaning in the darkness to please shoot him and end his pain. Most of us were too scared to get out of our foxholes and crawl around. There were Jap snipers among the trees. But finally somebody couldn't stand it any longer, and he crawled out and got the wounded man to aid. But he died before it was light."

Such stories as this, also, had helped to prepare me mentally for my first combat. They were in my mind when, at 0600 on D-day morning, I followed John Wheaton into the halftrack in our hold and began describing into our recording machine what was happening.*

Ours was the first vehicle to be lifted from the hold. While Seabees put braces beneath the halftrack and attached them to lines from the winches, Wheaton and I knelt in the vehicle and prepared to be hoisted topside. Marines huddled about the hold, smoking cigarettes and watching us.

The halftrack was filled with gear: packs, blanket rolls, ammunition boxes, machine guns, water cans, camouflage netting, and weapons and paraphernalia that would be needed on the beach. Our recording equipment was lashed in among the gear, and Wheaton squatted on a pile of packs to operate the machine. He was going to stay in the vehicle all the way in. When we reached the reef, I would have to get out and

* See Appendix for the actual transcript of the recording made during the landing.

wade along with the other men in the outfit. That was because the halftrack, lumbering across the 450-yard-wide reef,
would be too big a target for the Japs. Besides Wheaton, only
the driver and radioman-machine-gunner would be allowed
to ride in the vehicle. The rest of us would have to stay as far
away from the halftrack as possible.

With a clatter and banging, we were slowly lifted out of
the hold and swung over the side of the transport, down into
a waiting LCM—a small tank lighter. As soon as we were
secured in the tiny bobbing craft, a cargo net was dropped
down to us, and we heard a voice roar through the transport's
loud-speaker: "First trip of boats! Man your debarkation
nets."

The next instant Marines poured down the net into the
boat. Thirty-two men, including the crew of the halftrack
and members of the Weapons Company headquarters, were
assigned to the LCM. They half-fell from the lower rungs
of the net into the boat and scrambled to assigned positions
around the LCM's bulkheads. A trailer filled with flame-
throwers and communications gear, and a rubber boat, were
also lowered to us. The trailer was attached to the halftrack
to be towed across the reef. The rubber boat was for any
casualties we might have. Two of our men were assigned to
pull it, once we left the LCM and began to wade.

When all our men were down the net, we pulled away from
the side of the transport and joined a group of small LCVPs
—Higgins boats—that were circling near by in a rendezvous
area. We could see sailors and Seabees waving goodbye to us
from the deck of the transport. Some of them were standing
watch in gun tubs, ready for a possible Jap air raid. One man
hallooed across the water at us: "Get some Japs for me!"

H-hour was to be at eight-thirty. Our first waves would
come from the LSTs which were standing close off shore.
While they were landing we would gradually move toward
the beach, passing from one line of control to another. These
control lines were spaced several thousand yards apart. Small

craft were at each line, organizing and directing the boats of each wave, so that they moved on schedule and in an orderly fashion toward the section of the beach on which they would land their men.

The transports were about seven miles off the beachhead. As we moved away from the big ships, we could see Marines of the next wave flowing down the cargo nets like brown waterfalls into more landing boats.

From our first rendezvous area, Guam was just a purple smudge on the horizon. Between us and the island were our warships, still shelling the Jap positions. We could see orange flashes shooting out from the big guns. As we moved nearer the island, we could smell the powder and make out the fog of smoke that hung over the water off the beachhead.

We passed all kinds of ships, anchored like an armada off the Jap beach. There were big, green-painted landing ships, repair vessels, communications boats. They flew colored pennants, each of which signified something to our coxswains trying to guide our boats in toward the correct beach.

One man said the scene reminded him of a boat race back home. "It's as if we were coming up to the starting line," he said.

Just after eight-thirty the radioman in our boat leaned over his walkie-talkie and pressed his headphones tighter against his ears.

"First wave ashore," he yelled.

We gathered around him, as he listened to the radio conversations between units on the beach and the command ship. After a moment, he looked up and smiled.

"Casualties light."

No one said anything. The men looked at each other and nodded.

We passed a battleship, then two destroyers, shelling the island. The noise around us was thunderous.

One man shouted into the ear of the Marine beside him: "You think anything's left on the island?"

The other man yelled back: "Tell you when I get there!"

Major Gammon moved from one man to the next, shouting final directions: "Soon as we hit the beach, get around the halftrack as security!"

We had been thoroughly briefed before and knew that our first job was to get to a prearranged location, set up a command post, and await orders from the regimental commander.

About ten minutes after the first wave landed, our group of boats reached the line of transfer. We waited while infantrymen in Higgins boats around us transferred into amphibious tractors that would take them across the reef. Because a tractor couldn't carry our halftrack, we would have to get out of our LCM at the lip of the reef and wade in the open, while the infantrymen in tractors clanked over the coral beside us.

We could see Guam clearly. The beachhead, which lay between two points, smoked from end to end. The points, jutting out toward the reef, seemed to be on fire. The more prominent one, Adelup Point, on our left, was topped by a concrete building that looked like a Spanish-type hacienda; the Japs had converted it into a fort.

When the infantrymen in our wave had completed their transfer, a control boat raced up beside us and gave our coxswain an order to follow him. The coxswain for the first time during the morning put on his helmet. Another Navy man in the boat pulled a canvas hood from a machine gun and took his position behind a steel shield. The coxswain gunned the motor of our LCM, and we shot forward. On each side of us, the amphibious tractors churned even with us, their radio aerials bent backward like long fishing rods. We could see placards held up in each boat, showing the wave and the boat number. The tractors were low in the water. We could scarcely see the Marines huddling in them. Only their big pot helmets stuck up above the bulkheads.

Ahead, we suddenly saw explosions in the water. Big shells were landing near the reef. For the first time, we began to hear the chatter of machine guns. We got down low in our boat and looked up at the clear, blue sky.

"Lots of noise!" a corporal shouted.

"And it ain't a maneuver," another man answered.

"It's like Scollay Square on a Saturday night," a man from Boston yelled.

Some of the men laughed. We felt our stomach muscles tighten and relax in spasms.

Our LCM paused suddenly, and we realized we were at the line of departure—the last line. The control boat signaled to us, then turned back for the next wave.

"We're going in," the coxswain yelled. "Get ready to hit the reef."

The men crouched and pulled back the bolts of their rifles and carbines. A clicking ran through the boat as the weapons were cocked. We roared forward. Somebody called, "Good luck!"

The next instant we hit the reef. A shudder ran through the boat. The ramp crashed down on the coral and the coxswain yelled to get going. One by one, the Marines stepped out into the water. The driver of the halftrack pressed his accelerator, and the vehicle ground down the ramp and dipped with a splash onto the reef. The rest of us followed, jumping into the warm water.

It was difficult wading across the reef. The coral was sharp and slippery, and the water in some places was ankle-deep, in others almost hip-deep. One man fell and picked himself up quickly, looking around and laughing nervously. The air was full of a loud, composite noise, a roar made up of the sounds of shelling, small-arms fire, the halftrack's motor, and the rattle of amphibious tractors over the coral near us. The beach was wrapped in smoke. In places we saw shattered palm trees, looking like burnt telephone poles. Explosions came from our left. One man shouted and pointed: through the smoke obscuring Adelup Point we could see orange flashes— Jap guns firing straight at us, sweeping in flanking fire across the reef. The Point still hadn't been knocked out, despite our naval bombardment. We looked up. American planes were diving over the Point and the looming hills back of the beach. The hills rose above the smoke. They seemed to go straight up—directly behind the beach.

On the sand we saw a man get up and run; the smoke swallowed him. In the water to our right an amphibious tractor was burning. Jap mortar shells threw up fountains of water near it. Ahead of us were more fountains. We would have to go through them. We felt lonely.

"Hey!" I shouted, trying to laugh. "Don't leave me alone."

A man near by turned and grinned. I saw small splashes in the water almost next to him. I gripped the small hand microphone I was carrying and tried to concentrate on what I was saying.

"Machine-gun fire!" somebody yelled. And another called: "Spread out!"

The word passed from man to man. Instinctively, the men moved farther apart. We were spread over an area almost one hundred yards wide. Some of the men, a hundred yards ahead of me, went down to their necks in the water, trying to hide under the surface. They held their rifles above their heads; then they got up again and pushed through the water.

A fountain of spray shot up near me. We could hear the high crack of rifles. The halftrack paused suddenly. I looked at the wire connecting my microphone with the recording machine in the vehicle. I felt like dropping the microphone and getting farther away from halftrack; if it was going to get stuck, I didn't want to be near it. A man who had been swimming in front of the vehicle, looking for boulders and potholes, stood up and waved the driver in a circle around him. The halftrack lurched ahead again.

The trailer suddenly turned over and dragged through the water. Someone yelled to the halftrack driver to stop, but he couldn't hear. Communications gear fell into the water and floated around us. A man was hit—our first one. Two men pulled him to the rubber boat and laid him across it. Two others on the opposite side grabbed the injured man's arms and helped lay him down evenly. Another man was hit, and sank in the water. Major Gammon yelled to get him. "Don't let him drown!" he shouted.

A third man, and a fourth, went down. Bullets were whistling around us. A splash of water hid two men from view. When the spray fell, one of the men spun around backward, his neck bleeding. The other man caught him. By now the rubber boat was full of wounded, and a Marine walking beside it was trying to give one of the men a sulfa pill. Another injured man was hanging onto the trailer with both arms, dragging through the water. He had dropped his weapon, and his face was drawn with pain as he tried to hang on.

We were almost on the beach. We could see Marines lying on the sand. Other men were moving cautiously among the debris. At the edge of the beach a man lay on his back, his feet in the water, his eyes open. Blood was pouring out of him.

Three halftracks were piled on the sand near us. Marines were crouched behind them. An amphibious tractor backed out past us. Its placard hung crazily over the side where the members of a preceding wave had dropped it.

Our halftrack came to an abrupt stop. It was half on the beach and half in the water. There was no place to go. The preceding waves were still in the tangled rubbish of the shattered coconut trees at the top of the beach. We saw Major Gammon scramble up the sand and fall flat behind an uprooted coconut tree. The rest of us crouched around the halftrack. Behind us, we could see another wave coming in. Marines were wading across the coral, trying to keep as low in the water as possible without wetting their weapons. They were spread out around another halftrack. Jap bullets cut through the water. One man was carrying an injured Marine over his shoulder.

We heard heavy explosions near us, and a spray of coral drummed on the halftrack. Major Gammon began to shout:

THE CLIFF ABOVE THE GUAM BEACHHEAD. On top of this cliff, before we had rigged the block and tackle stretcher, Gunnery Sergeant Margolis died.

AFTER THE BANZAI CHARGE. On top of Banzai Ridge, Guam, the morning after the fanatical Jap night attack.

"Get the hell away from the halftracks. They'll be hit.
They'll blow up!"

We had to end our recording.

Wheaton snapped off the machine and jumped out of the
vehicle; we huddled behind it, the water lapping our feet. All
around us, men knelt and lay, most of them bleeding. One,
who was hysterical, was being held by a corpsman, while
with his free hand the corpsman tried to press a battle dressing against the forehead of a man who lay mostly under the
halftrack. Two other Marines with bloody dungarees
watched him, their eyes wide and staring. Another man ran
into our group, stumbled over one of the wounded Marines,
and shouted at no one in particular: "Jug's killed! Jug's
killed!" He looked at us wildly. "The Major says to get out
of here. The halftrack's drawing mortars. Get up to the coconuts!" Then he turned and bolted back up the sand.

We helped the corpsman for a moment. Then he dropped
the compress on the man half lying under the halftrack. "He's
dead," he said calmly.

One of the Marines took the hysterical man and guided him
away. They walked around the halftrack, moving as nonchalantly as if they were on a Sunday stroll, and disappeared
from sight.

One by one we dashed up the beach. From the hills, from
their hundreds of observation and firing positions, the Japs
looked down on us and let us have it. They had recovered
from the initial shock of the prelanding bombardment and
had made up their minds that this was to be our main invasion.
Our first waves, which had landed without much opposition,
had got halfway up the hills overlooking the beach. But the
rest of us were in trouble. The Jap fire was increasing in in-
tensity each minute. Enemy artillery and mortars were being
brought from other parts of the island. They were being
registered in. Machine guns, Nambus, and rifles were cracking at us from all the hills. We could hear the crashing of
mortar shells closer and closer. We could see the black foun-

tains going up on the beach, in the water, and among the coconut trees, and could hear the whistle of bullets flying past our heads. We didn't want to leave what seemed to be the shelter of the halftrack's steel body for the dash across the open. But the big vehicles were targets; one might be hit any moment.

Stumbling and sliding through the sand, we ran across the open, a distance of about fifteen yards. It seemed like a hundred. We fell scared and out of breath behind a sand dune and lay on our stomachs panting. Why were we still alive?— No time to think about it. The only thing was to stay alive. Save yourself. Don't raise up. Don't move. It was like Tarawa. Men crowded on the sand. When would it end? How would we get out of it?

We wondered suddenly whether this was any different from what men had undergone during every other amphibious landing in this war. We had sat at home comfortably and read about them—stories under a one-column head, impersonal stuff written at a rear base about our side: landing somewhere, moderate opposition, light casualties, progress made . . .

There was a terrific crash. Then another, like a house falling down. Sand and coral rained through the air like ashes. A moaning started, high, like a baby whimpering. The odor of blood and cordite filled our nostrils.

A man slid past us, almost crying. His foot was a pulpy mass. "Where's a corpsman?" he sobbed. "Where's a goddamned corpsman?"

Somebody motioned back to the water. "Down there, Joe."

The man with the injured foot paused and wiped his nose, then dragged on. "Gotta get a corpsman," he cried. "Gotta get a corpsman. There's boys dying back there."

We knew that at home somebody would soon be getting the news and saying to somebody else: "I see we landed on another little island."

III

Pinned Down

DURING our first moments on Guam we experienced brief but unforgettable moments of comradeship with men we scarcely knew and might never see again. It was the way of combat. The loneliness in the face of such peril made us reach for and grasp companionship. Even the planes above us and the tanks around us, firing at the enemy who was trying to kill us, became personalities on our side, allies helping us get out of the tight spot we were in.

The men on the bloody beach at Guam that morning were all part of our team. Most of us had never seen each other before. Some of us were casual shipboard acquaintances. But somehow, as we tried to organize ourselves under all that Jap fire, it seemed as if we were bound together by ties of brotherhood we had never felt before. A familiar face suddenly became an old friend; an old friend was something infinitely dearer and more precious than anything else in the world at that moment. There was nothing one man wouldn't do for another, even if he had never seen him before.

For almost half an hour there was no place for us to go. We couldn't get the halftrack up on the beach, and we couldn't move ahead. Advance platoons of the 3d Marines were part way up the hill in front of us. But they were completely exposed on the bare slope, and the Japs were subjecting them—as they were all of us—to a murderous fire. There was little anyone could do in our outfit but seek cover and wait.

I lay behind a sand dune next to two men I had known slightly on the transport. We had been in the same LCM coming ashore, but we had lost track of each other wading across the reef. Now, after dashing up the beach from the halftrack, I found myself beside them on the sand.

One of them was on his back, breathing heavily and staring at the sky. His lips were moving almost mechanically in prayer. The other man was lying on his stomach, his arms out ahead of him and his head raised slightly. He was leafing through a small overseas edition of a news magazine that someone in a wave ahead had probably dropped from his pack as he ran across the sand. When he saw me, he laughed and motioned toward his companion. "Look at him pray!" he shouted. "He thinks it will save him now."

He talked fast and loudly, almost as if he didn't know what he was saying. But he was trying to joke—the best thing to do with all the steel flying around us. The other man wasn't listening to anything. His lips kept moving rapidly. Finally he rolled his eyes sideways and saw me.

"Hi!" he exclaimed. "Swell seeing you." Then he went on with his prayer.

A few moments later Major Gammon slid past us. Mortar shells were bursting near us again.

"Get up among the coconut trees till we can organize our CP," the Major hollered. "More cover."

Several of us crawled slowly behind a cluster of roots of fallen coconut trees and looked back at the reef. Another wave was coming in. I saw Dale DeWitt, my shipboard acquaintance from Beverly Hills, plow in through the water and emerge on the sand, puffing and looking around bewilderedly. He glanced at the other men in his machine-gun section and ordered them down on the sand. It made me feel good to see DeWitt hit the beach safely.

Wheaton joined me and pointed out that our artillery outfit was landing already. We could see them coming in on amphibious tractors. No guns—just a reconnaissance party to select positions for the guns and CPs. As we watched them, there was a sudden tremendous burst of flame that almost seared our eyes, followed by a crash and a rumble. One of the amtracs had hit a mine in the water and had blown up. Two figures in black rags bolted away from the flames and fell into the water. Men near the water's edge ran to the tractor. The next instant a row of bullets splattered against the coconut trees over our heads. We ducked.

"I wish I was in West Virginia," Wheaton yelled.

We crawled a few feet through the matting of coconut fronds and debris trying to find a hole. When we discovered one, and slid in, we were half on top of a rifleman who was huddled in it with his knees drawn up against his chest. We lay there for ten minutes not saying a word. Dive bombers flew over us, so low that it seemed as if they would crash into the hills looming above us. As they came, they hurled rockets and fired machine-gun bullets into the tops of the ridges. It was a terrible racket, like the crashing of cymbals. Every so often a flight of planes dropped bombs, seeming to unload them directly over us. We looked up and watched the bombs fall straight down on us, and, just when we started to swear, they drifted sideways and pounded into the slopes of the hills.

"My God!" Wheaton exclaimed irritably. "I wish they'd go play somewhere else."

We were cramped, in that tiny foxhole. The rifleman finally lit a cigarette and offered each of us one. "Where you from?" he said.

I told him Washington, D. C.

He opened his eyes wide and grinned. "Me too." He told me his address. We were almost neighbors. "This is one for the books," he said. After a while, he crushed out his cigarette. "I'd better get going," he said. "I was in the third wave. I lost my outfit. They must be somewhere up ahead."

"Take care," Wheaton said.

We watched the rifleman slide up out of the hole and across

the debris. He pushed his rifle out ahead of him, stumbled to his feet, and ran through the brush and out of sight.

Other men went past us: riflemen, machine gunners, BAR men with Brownings, grenadiers, and other assault Marines organized now into squads and teams with specific jobs to do. Some of the men we knew, and we yelled to them as they passed us. When DeWitt and his machine gunners went by, he paused and looked down at us.

"What are you hiding from?" he called.

Just then a bullet splattered against a coconut tree a foot away. DeWitt fell flat. He raised himself slowly and looked at us. "I'm going up where it's safe," he said. "It's not healthy back here." And he continued on to the front.

On the beach we could see Marines with red squares painted on their dungaree pants and jackets—unloaders, who had just landed. They stuck big placards in the sand showing where to bring in the different supplies. Each type of supply had a different symbol painted on a placard: rations, ammunition, water, etc. Bullets were still hitting on the sand and mortar shells in the water, and the men were jumping around as if they thought they could dodge the flying missiles. The amphibious tractor that had struck the mine was still burning. Down the beach a group of Seabees were trying to raise a small American flag on the shattered trunk of a coconut tree. One man was shinnying up the tree on the side toward the water. As the trunk bent out towards the water, it was a hard job; the Seabee was practically hanging on his back.

By noon the rifle units in our sector were several hundred yards inland and up the slopes of the hills. The ridges began rising about two hundred yards in from the beach and, in some places, went several hundred yards almost straight up. Behind them, like the ripples of giant green waves, were higher hills, undulating inland in a procession of ridges and valleys.

Presently Major Gammon and the other officers of the Weapons Company managed to set up a CP in a length of a

Jap trench that ran through the coconut grove. Our first problem was getting the halftracks up on the road. Enemy rifle and machine-gun fire had by this time decreased. Our squads had slowly been finding and wiping out the nearest Jap nests. But from the tops of the hills the enemy were still shelling us with mortars and artillery. A little after noon, with the help of a bulldozer that plowed a path through the sand dunes and debris, we got four halftracks across the coconut strip and onto the road. The halftrack with which I had landed was immediately given orders to join the attack on Adelup Point—the Point that had been firing at us when we landed. Word had come to us that there was still a battery of Jap 77s amid all the rubble on the Point, sending enveloping fire across the reef at our forces still landing.

The halftrack set off on its mission, while Wheaton and I remained behind to help establish the CP in the sandy trench. A couple of minutes later, we heard a loud explosion and a rumble to our left. It sounded louder than a mortar-shell explosion, and we thought a land mine had gone off. The radio operator of the halftrack came running back. He was wringing his hands excitedly. "We hit something," he cried. "The halftrack's wrecked!"

Then the driver stumbled back. His dungarees were torn, and he was suffering from shock. We couldn't understand anything he said.

Several of us moved along the road, dodging from tree to tree to find out what had happened. About two hundred yards down the road on the way to Adelup Point we saw the halftrack. Its right front wheel was shattered; it had either hit a land mine or suffered a direct mortar-shell burst. Seven of our men were lying on the ground around it—all the fellows with whom I had landed, except the driver and the radio operator, the only ones who had escaped.

None of the men was dead, though several were critically injured. Corpsmen were already at work. We helped get the wounded back to the beach, where amphibious tractors evacuated them. Then we abandoned the halftrack and returned to the CP. Our first sergeant shook his head sadly. "Soon we won't have anybody left," he said. He and a Navy corpsman went over their rosters, making notes on the outfit's casualties.

"We didn't have one casualty all through the Bougainville campaign," the first sergeant said. "And look how many we've got already. And the first day isn't even through."

A Pfc was standing guard at the CP. "I want to thank you for saving my life," he said to me.

"How?" I asked.

"Remember when we were wading across the reef? I was ahead of you and you yelled to me not to leave you behind. I turned to hear what you were saying, and just then a bullet hit in the water where I would have been if I hadn't paused."

"All right," I said. "Now it's your turn to save mine."

He laughed. "The worst is over now," he said.

But the worst wasn't over.

The Japs continued to shell us from above. And, as they brought more of their equipment from other parts of the island, their fire grew more intense. Every time a mortar shell landed, it seemed that one of our outfit was a casualty. We would hear a blast, duck, then look up and call: "Who got it this time?" After a moment, down along the trench would come a frantic call for a corpsman. Sometimes the blast would be close and men would go down in front of our eyes, hit by pieces of flying steel. Being hit soon began to seem not so serious—it was too commonplace. There would be an explosion, and a man to whom we had been talking a few minutes before would be lying in the sand on his back, sucking the air in between his teeth and holding onto his arm. The wound was usually a little black gash or a hole with blood around it—not much worse than a big splinter. The corpsmen would dress the wound and the man would be helped away, down to the beach and off the island. He would be through with the battle—through with the misery and tension. Eventually we began referring to "million-dollar wounds"—wounds that

*THEY WERE DRUNK WHEN THEY DIED. Some of the Jap
dead on top of Banzai Ridge the morning after the wild assault.*

JAP CAVE AT GUAM. Marines call on Japs, hiding within, to surrender. When the enemy refused, the Marines sealed the cave.

would get us out of the battle and yet not maim or disfigure us. An injury in the arm or leg, for instance, was a "million-dollar wound."

Late in the afternoon the man who had thanked me for saving his life learned personally that the worst wasn't over. A mortar fragment ripped into him and he was evacuated.

Toward evening the beach was filled with a terrible odor. When I helped bring in water cans from a short way up the beach, I discovered why: our sector was filled with dead men still unburied. Shore parties were working over the bodies as fast as they could under the enemy fire, but it was a difficult job to stay alive yourself, let alone identify a corpse and dig a grave in the beach for it. Near our dugout were five bodies laid out on the sand side by side—the men who had been killed in the amphibious tractor that had exploded. The tractor itself was upended on the sand near the water's edge. Beside it under the shelter of a sand dune was a beach evacuation station, run by Naval corpsmen and doctors from the transports that had unloaded on our section of the beach. The station was crowded with wounded men who had been streaming from the hillside all day. Most of them were already dressed and tagged, waiting for amphibious tractors to take them out to the transports and hospital ships. There were many stretcher cases, some already dead, some fighting for life. Corpsmen and less seriously wounded men knelt beside the stretchers, holding up plasma bottles. In one corner against the tractor was a pile of bloodstained stretchers. Beside the stretchers sat a small group of men suffering from combat fatigue. They shook and quivered like frightened puppies, and their staring eyes were bloodshot. Every noise made them jump in terror. When a tractor came in to take aboard a load of wounded, the explosions from its exhaust sent the men sprawling out in the sand and cringing as though they were trying to find shelter from a shell. A corpsman who looked about sixteen years old moved among them, patting them quietly and tenderly on the back and trying to reassure them.

Night found our position precarious in the sector in which we were dug. A strong Jap counterattack might easily drive into us in the darkness and either cut us up or throw us off the beach. Also, we were told to prepare for possible Jap counter-landings on the same beach on which we had landed during the day. To repel such a Jap move, amphibious tractors were drawn up at the water's edge behind us.

None of us slept that night. We sat up in the trench, facing in different directions and listening for strange noises. There were many mosquitoes, and we wore our headnets under our helmets. Each man was responsible as a guard in his section of the trench for two hours. Occasionally a field telephone rang in our dugout, passing on orders or telling us the situation. Major Gammon answered each time in a voice hardly above a whisper. Throughout the night there was firing in the hills above us. Illumination flares hung over us, fired from our warships to reveal any Jap movements. The flares lit up the terrain and made every moving shape an easy target.

At about five in the morning the 'phone rang. The Major answered it in a husky voice. Then he hung up and wiped his mouth anxiously. "Pass the word to stay down when it gets light," he said. "We're surrounded."

Our hearts beat wildly. All night we had been awake without seeing or hearing the enemy. Now we were surrounded. This was the Jap enemy.

With the first rays of light we realized that the message was correct—though the word "surrounded" made the situation sound more ominous than it was. There *were* Japs among us, in the coconut trees and in holes out on the beach. They began firing around us. The high cracks of their rifles were close. But there were only a few of them, fighting as individuals, here and there. They were well hidden and fired only when one of us gave them a target to shoot at.

At first we didn't know what to do. We couldn't see them. Yet whenever we raised a little, a shot would snap at us. Finally we began to spot them. We fired back and threw hand grenades. By six in the morning we had killed a half-dozen Japs. We began to show ourselves, and there were no more potshots.

During the morning I decided to look for our Division CP and deliver the record we had made of our landing. I left the Weapons Company and moved through the coconut strip toward our right flank.

The 3d Marines had formed the left flank of the beachhead, so I had a long way to go to reach the other flank near where Division Headquarters was supposed to be. I passed through the headquarters units of outfit after outfit, all of which were fighting up in the hills. The farther I went, the better our progress inland seemed to be, and consequently the less firing there was on the beaches.

I found the Division CP dug in among the dirt banks of a narrow stream in a glen shaded by coconut and breadfruit trees. A dressing station was set up by the side of the stream, and the water was running red. The CP had taken a beating the previous night from Jap mortar shells. Even now enemy shells were falling.

The news that our combat correspondents were sending in to Headquarters showed that every outfit had "taken it." In the 9th Marines, in fact, all of our correspondents had been casualties; one had been killed and two wounded. One of the latter was the correspondent who had joined us in the Marshalls after having been flown by error to Saipan. He had now been hit in the foot and been evacuated. His career was probably one of the fullest for such a brief period overseas—two battles in a couple of weeks.

I gave my recordings to a staff officer for shipment to the United States and asked how the fighting was going.

"It's going fine everywhere," he said, "except in your area."

It was true. We were talking in a spot about five hundred yards inland from the beach. And the fighting was so much farther in on that flank that we could barely hear machine guns and rifles. Except for the occasional mortar shells hurled from enemy positions in the 3d Marine sector, we felt completely secure.

At the CP I heard some of the stories that were coming back from the front lines of the other outfits. Many of them concerned the legendary character of our Division, "Slug" Marvin, who had gotten the clean clothes for his flame-throwing unit in the Marshalls. Marvin was supposed to have roared like a bull hundreds of yards out ahead of our front lines all through the first day, leading the 21st Marines in the center of the line. The great progress made by the 21st, according to the stories, was achieved in part by Marvin's aggressiveness, which took hold of and inspired units all around him. He had personally burned many caves and blown up several Jap pillboxes. Wounded men coming back from the front told of having seen him standing in the open and shrieking: "Come out and fight, you bastards!"

The first night Marvin killed a Jap with a shovel and slept on him. The story went that Marvin saw a Jap foxhole with a dead Jap in it and decided to sleep there rather than dig another foxhole. As he started to throw in some dirt to cover the dead Jap, the Jap stirred and sat up—he had only pretended to be dead. So Marvin hit him with his shovel until he really killed him, then threw some dirt on him and went to sleep. He said the next morning that he had slept well until rigor mortis had set in on the Jap; then it had been uncomfortable.

The second day of the fighting, according to another story, Marvin killed some Japs with a hatchet. Everyone knew that "Slug" had brought along a hatchet with which to try to kill Japs. On Bougainville he had actually scalped some Japs with a machete. He had thrown a grenade into a pillbox, then rushed in the rear entrance and, taking the dazed occupants by surprise, had scalped them. It was now said that he had done the same thing on Guam with a hatchet.

Another story told at the time concerned a master gunnery sergeant and an incident that had occurred on top of a cliff which the 21st Marines had scaled the first day. One of our machine guns on top of the cliff had come under Jap fire that was concealed from our view. One after another, our gunners on that weapon were knocked out by accurate enemy fire. Volunteers who crawled up and tried to man the gun met the same fate. Suddenly a wizened old regular named Israel Margolis appeared from nowhere and began crawling to the gun.

Margolis was forty-eight years old and a naturalized American. He had fought in the Russian army in the last war. After the Russian Revolution he had somehow joined the A.E.F. and had then returned to the United States, been naturalized, and joined the Marine Corps. He had two loves: the United States and the Marine Corps. In the Corps he was an ordnance expert. He should have been in the rear, repairing weapons and supervising the distribution of ammunition. No one knew how he got up to the top of that cliff. But he had probably seen the wounded streaming back all day and had figured that he might be needed.

He had no sooner reached the "hot" machine gun on the cliff, however, than the Japs got him. A corpsman dragged the little man back to the edge of the cliff and tried to dress his wound. There was no way of getting Margolis down the cliff. Seabees and engineers were rigging a block-and-tackle to sling a portable stretcher, but it wouldn't be ready for hours. Meanwhile Margolis was dying.

The corpsman knelt by the side of the older man and asked him if there was anything he wanted. Margolis stared hard a moment and nodded. "Please," he said in a hoarse whisper, "sing *God Bless America*." In a breaking voice, with the noise of mortar shells and bullets around him, the corpsman sang to the old Marine. Other wounded men gathered around and gazed at the ground. Some cried unashamedly. Finally the tough little professional soldier died.

Before leaving the Division CP and returning to the Weapons Company I learned that there was to be an all-out attack on the hill holding us up on our flank. I left hurriedly, hoping to see the attack. It was a strange and unpleasant feeling, walking back along the beach road, back to the enemy and the bullets and shells. I went no farther inland, but the more I walked, the closer I approached action. Soon I passed dead men lying in shellholes, among battered concrete foundations of buildings. It was the village of Asan. Not a structure was standing, but among the ruins was a bird house set on a pole—quite undamaged. There was already a lot of traffic on the road: tanks, amphibious tractors, jeeps, trucks. In places they moved quickly to avoid snipers' bullets from the hills. Men huddled behind trees and bushes and shouted at the drivers: "There's a sniper in there! You better go fast!"

In crossing those openings, men on foot stayed on the beach side of vehicles, trotting alongside them for the length of the dangerous area. There were also mines still in the road, cardboard signs showing where some of these were. Every so often, however, a vehicle would hit an undiscovered one. There would be a dull explosion and a lot of smoke. The vehicle would halt suddenly, and the driver and passengers (if any) would end up on their backs along the roadside with bloody, blackened faces and hands, and torn, charred clothing. The Japs had used a variety of types of mines, including aerial bombs and torpedo warheads, in the road.

When I reached the Weapons Company, the preparations for the all-out attack on the hillside were already under way. Planes were diving in in repeated waves, dropping bombs and rockets, and machine-gunning the top of the hill. Cruisers and destroyers were pounding the ridge crest with big stuff from way out. LCIs at the lip of the reef were hurling flights of rockets point-blank. Our artillery was thundering in from the right flank; and from the road, where we were, our half-tracks were shooting up with their 75s. Giant bursts of flame, followed by clouds of brown and yellow smoke, rose from the top of the hill. Flash after flash showed direct hits—all on an area a few hundred yards square. It was incredible that anyone could live through the pounding.

Yet they did. Somehow Japs, armed with machine guns, rifles, and portable grenade dischargers which we called knee mortars, were holed in up there and living through the shattering barrage. The din, even to us at the base of the hill, was ear-splitting. We lay in our trench and looked up, as if we had front-row seats at a mighty and terrible drama. For a while, as the planes kept coming, and the guns kept pounding, and the bursts kept skyrocketing on the hilltop, we thought we had everything our own way.

Then, when our barrage paused momentarily, we saw that it wasn't so. There on the brown hillside, burned bare of grass by our planes before the landing, our troops tried to take advantage of the barrage and struggle upward a few yards, only to be mowed down in the open by men who had lived through something we couldn't believe human beings could stand. Wave after wave of green-dungareed Marines, standing out in bold relief against the brown hillside, crawled and scrambled up, only to be hit and sent rolling back by machine guns, hand grenades, and mortar shells.

It was dreadful watching it, and there was nothing we could do. The planes came in again, and the big guns fired some more. Smoke bombs were dropped in front of the Jap positions. Our men crawled up the hillside on all fours. We could see the dead and wounded; they stayed behind, not moving. Suddenly the smoke blew away, and the Japs poured down more fire. The Marine forms froze to the ground. There was some cover up there—little mounds, rocks, indentations in the earth. We could see an officer crawling slowly among his men, whispering to some of them, trying to do it without too much motion. We could see a corpsman risking his life to crawl to a group of wounded men. Almost there, he stiffened. A Jap machine gunner had caught him in the open.

Near dusk the men tried again. There was another barrage and more smoke bombs. A lieutenant and six men, higher up than the others, rose to their feet and charged to the crest. Down below, we saw them and cheered. Other men rose and followed. A burst of orange fire came through the smoke. A wave of our men fell down, some tumbling, some sliding back from where they had come. The rest sought cover behind mounds.

That night our men lay out on the slope where they were trapped. From below, our artillery and halftracks fired continuously at the ridge crest. Our halftracks were drawn up on the beach road in front of our CP with orders to fire so many rounds every fifteen minutes. We who were living in the trench and foxholes on the beach weren't so keen about having the halftracks right there, because they would draw return enemy mortar fire. But the situation in the hills was serious. We scooped out side hollows in the trench as added protection against flying shell fragments and spent another sleepless night.

The next day the fight continued. Many of our men went up as reinforcements, and when the survivors of the previous day's attacks came down they told us what it had been like. Most of the previous day they had simply lain on the open slope in the broiling sun, scarcely able to make a move without attracting Jap fire. Tortured by thirst, when the water in their canteens gave out they had drunk the water out of their machine guns. All around them were their dead and wounded buddies, and there was nothing they could do for them. They couldn't get to many of the seriously wounded men, and some had slowly died in the open. The smell of the dead and the gathering flies had almost driven the others crazy. The attack before dusk had been like a Godsend simply because it had meant something to do—a chance to get out of the maddening situation. But many more of them had died in that rush, just as many were still dying.

The third day on the beach, the stalemate was finally broken. Seabees and engineers completed a rough, bulldozed road up a steep draw leading to the left flank of the hill. Behind tanks, reinforcements went up and flanked the Jap positions. On the other side, units of the 9th and 21st Marines

AGANA, CAPITAL OF GUAM. The Third Marines move through what is left of the city in which we thought we would have our first real "liberty."

INTO THE GUAM BOONDOCKS. A bulldozer stayed up with us to cut paths over which chow and supply trucks
could come

also closed in. The kill was made late in the afternoon after another withering barrage. A team of our engineer demolitions men were among the first to reach the crest. They came up the right flank. Pausing near the top during one of our barrages, they noticed that the moment our heavy fire started, the Japs would leave a machine-gun position and duck into a cave; and the instant the barrage was over, they would spring out again and man the machine gun. The engineers waited for another one of our barrages. When it came, they watched the Japs disappear; then they sprang up, grabbed the machine gun, pulled it down the crest, turned it around, and waited for the barrage to end. This time, when the Japs returned, the engineers mowed them down with their own gun, then stormed up the crest to meet Marines from the opposite flank.

On the hilltop we found a maze of spider pits (round foxholes with covers), trenches and dugouts. The Japs had been able to weather our bombardments in the dugouts and caves that filled a coral outcropping. The whole ridge crest was covered with broken Jap bodies. What our bombardments hadn't done, the final attacking waves accomplished, using hand grenades and bayonets.

We were now in a position to broaden our beachhead and push inland. On the right flank the 9th Marines were sweeping around Apra Harbor to try to join the beachhead established several miles away by the 1st Provisional Marine Brigade. In the center the 21st Marines, who had been marking time waiting for the 3d to come up, were impatient to push ahead. And on our flank the 3d Marines, weakened by heavy casualties, were anxious to free their side of the beachhead from Jap fire and to secure their part of the reef so that supplies could be unloaded.

What we didn't look forward to, as we prepared to push across the high ground of Guam, was a Jap counterattack—a banzai charge.

IV

Banzai!

O<small>N</small> D plus four, Wheaton and I were transferred to Division headquarters. Our recording equipment had taken a lot of punishment in the sand and debris of the landing beach, and we needed time to repair it. The record we had made of the landing was flown back to America, but it arrived ten days after D-day and aroused only mild interest. According to the radio stations, it had lost its topical value. The battle for Guam was, from the news perspective back home, just a battle for "another little island"—good for a few days' headlines.

On Guam, however, it was another story. Some of the fiercest moments of the struggle were still ahead of us. Our Division CP was in an amphitheater near the shore, in an area that lay beyond the right flank of our original beachhead. The amphitheater was formed by towering hills and coral bluffs. The open (or shore) side was bounded by a road. It was a fairly secure spot, guarded by rings of MPs and free from Jap mortar fire. Here, General Turnage and his staff set up tents from which to direct the deepening of our beachhead.

Our line was now many thousand yards long, and that it was a thin line was no secret. We were only one division, and we had no reinforcements. We had to push and keep pushing; and the more we pushed, the wider our perimeter became

54

and the more men we needed to hold it. We looked forward to the day when we would join the Provisional Brigade on the other beachhead. They had elements of the 77th Army Division with them as reinforcements. The 77th had begun landing its men late on D-day on that beachhead. As soon as we all joined, we could possibly count on reinforcements from the Army. Until then, however, we had to hold and deepen our perimeter alone.

During the night of July 25—D plus four—it rained. Toward morning we noticed the sound of gunfire coming closer to our Division CP. Then the guards up on the hills that formed the amphitheater began to shoot. At first there were just sporadic shots—a rifle or a carbine shot into the night. Then they came oftener. There were hand-grenade blasts, and the sudden bursts of BARs and machine guns.

Wheaton and I could hear men stirring in the holes around our foxhole. Occasionally a shot rang out very near to us. Then a hand grenade popped, so close that it might have been thrown by a man in a nearby hole. We peered cautiously over the lip of our foxhole and waited for a form to show itself.

Nothing happened, but by dawn the woods on top of the hills above us were resounding with shots. We got out of our holes carefully. Soon the word spread: the Japs had broken through. Several thousand of the enemy were behind our front lines, threatening all our rear units.

Things occurred then with terrible speed. Our artillery CP was overrun. Japs, carrying land mines and picric-acid charges around their belts, emerged from a draw and, throwing grenades, hit the artillery unit to which Wheaton and I had originally been attached. Our men fought back with rifles and hand grenades from the foxholes in which they had been sleeping. The Japs screamed in English (Staff Sergeant Jim Hague, one of our combat correspondents who was caught in the middle of the battle in his foxhole, reported that men that day heard Japs cry, "One, two, three, you can't catch me!") and charged into one of our machine-gun positions, taking the gun away from the crew. The Marines fought back with another machine gun and drove the Japs back up the draw. Lieutenant Rodgers, with whom we had sailed to Guam, collected a squad of men and boldly led it after the Japs. A flurry of shots from among some rocks stopped the group. One shot hit Rodgers, and he fell. The next moment there was an explosion; a hand grenade or a stick of dynamite—no one knew which—had hit the Lieutenant, and his body blew apart. Several other Marines were killed there, men who had been in our hold sailing to Guam.

While the artillerymen were fighting off the Japs, a second band of enemy rushed down another draw to appear suddenly at our Division hospital. The corpsmen and patients could hear firing coming nearer but thought nothing of it until a wounded man appeared, running at top speed and yelling: "The Japs are coming! The Japs are coming!"

There was no time to wonder how the Japs had broken so deeply into our rear. The corpsmen grabbed rifles and carbines and flung themselves behind cots and cartons of plasma and dressings. Some of the ambulatory patients hopped out of bed and ran for the beach. A cook, whose foot had been wounded the night before when he had been carrying ammunition, scrambled from his cot without a stitch of clothing on and hobbled as fast as he could to the shore. The Japs soon appeared at the hospital, screaming and throwing grenades. The corpsmen fired at them and tried to stop them. One corpsman killed seven Japs with a carbine. Patients inside the ward tents grabbed their weapons and joined the fight as hand-grenade fragments ripped into the canvas flaps. A doctor, in the middle of an operation, paused an instant, trying to decide what to do. The next moment two mortar bursts shredded the top of the surgery tent. The doctor ordered corpsmen to take up positions around the tent. Then he finished the operation.

It was a wild, swirling fight, but it was soon over. Reinforcements arrived from the Division CP and helped the corpsmen wipe out the Japs. Every enemy in sight was killed. But no one knew how many more were still behind our lines and out of sight. Reports from the front lines estimated that at least two thousand Japs had broken through during the night. There must still be almost that number wandering through the brush and hiding temporarily in caves behind our perimeter—a menace, since at any moment groups of them might attack other units, as they had attacked our artillery CP and the Division hospital.

Every Marine and Seabee on our beachhead was mobilized. Squads were formed to look for and attack the enemy that had broken through. All normal activity behind our front lines ceased. Cooks, drivers, clerks, telephone operators, unloaders on the reef—everyone available—went into the hills that morning to eliminate the threat to our beachhead.

Meanwhile we wondered what had happened. How had so many Japs gotten through, and when? The story, when it came down to us from the front lines, was the story of the first banzai charge our Division had ever met: a vicious, drunken, night counterattack designed to hurl us off of Guam and back into the sea.

The Japs' preparations for it had begun two nights before. That evening two of our PFCs, Joseph Basso and Russell Elushik, had been in an advanced foxhole in front of B Company, the 21st Marines. Basso, a husky former machinist, had been trying to get to sleep when Elushik, who was on guard, fired into the night with his automatic rifle. Basso leaped to his feet, to find the ground around the foxhole swarming with Japs. The two men stood back to back and fired as fast as they could at the enemy forms. The Japs, however, quickly overwhelmed them. The two men were dragged out of the foxhole and across the ground toward the Japanese lines. They struggled and yelled, but they were too far away from other Marines to make themselves heard.

At last Elushik, who weighed about two hundred pounds, twisted himself free and broke away. The Japs dragging

Basso let go and chased after Elushik. Basso scrambled breathlessly back to his foxhole and retrieved his automatic rifle. He saw the Japs overtake Elushik and knock the big man down. At the same moment, Basso emptied his rifle at the Japs, trying not to hit the forms on the ground. Several of the enemy fell. There was a sudden silence. A few Japs crawled stealthily away. Basso utilized the pause to scramble back to his own lines, get a man to cover him, and go back after Elushik. When he reached Elushik, the big man was still alive, despite the fact that his left hand had been cut off by a Jap saber, both his arms and legs had been broken, and he had a bayonet wound through his neck and back. Elushik and Basso were both evacuated that night. Elushik later died, but Basso, suffering from severe shock, recovered and rejoined his unit.

Nothing more was thought of the episode until two nights later when it became evident that the Jap raiding party had tried to take our men prisoners in order to obtain information. The enemy had chosen to hit the 21st Marines' sector in a counterattack and had needed an appraisal of our strength. Although they failed to secure information from Basso and Elushik, the Japs by themselves estimated our situation correctly. They narrowed the main force of their attack down to our weakest unit—the 1st Battalion of the 21st Marines. Here, in the very center of our whole beachhead line, no more than 250 men manned a position that ran for more than two thousand yards—a frontage normally requiring about 600 men. Company B, in the center of the 1st Battalion zone, was down to approximately 75 men out of an original landing strength of 217. The Marines, dug in on a ridge top a couple of miles from the shore, were organized in small knots to cover areas around them—islands of resistance, so to speak.

On the night of July 25 the Japs prepared to strike this sector.

That night, unaware of what lay ahead, our men on the ridge ate a dinner of cold K rations. The hours passed, and it began to pour and drizzle alternately. The Marines tucked

ponchos around themselves and squirmed sleepily in the mud.
Toward midnight one of the men on watch noticed that the
Japs were throwing a lot of grenades. On both sides of him,
other Marines were hurling their own grenades back into the
night. Many of these burst five and ten feet above the ground,
the fragments showering on the wet dirt.

At about three A.M. a rifleman named Martinez heard a swish-
ing of grass out ahead of him, like men moving about. Then
he noticed the *pang* of pieces of metal hitting each other and a
busy stirring in the darkness that made him uneasy. He peered
into the mist but was unable to see anything. Then, as he
listened, other things happened. A barrage of hand grenades
flew through the darkness and exploded behind him. They
kept coming, and he noticed mortar shells beginning to crash
more frequently on the ridge.

He woke the other two men in his foxhole. They had been
curled in their ponchos, and they got to their feet uncertainly.
At the same moment an orange signal flare shot up from the
Japanese lines. A singsong voice shouted into the night, and
an avalanche of screaming forms bounded suddenly into view.
With their bayonets gleaming in the light of sudden flares,
they charged toward the Marine foxholes, throwing grenades
and howling: "*Ban-zai-ai!*" like a pack of animals.

The Marines awoke with a start. Along the ridge, wet,
groggy men bolted to their feet and grabbed their weapons.
Grenades exploded like a crashing curtain against the onrush-
ing Japs. A man on a telephone yelled for uninterrupted flares,
and flickering lights began to hang in the air like giant overhead fires.

All along the line the enemy attack was on. Red tracer
bullets flashed through the blackness. Japanese orange signal
flares and American white illumination shells lit up the night
like the Fourth of July, silhouetting the running forms of the
enemy. On the right and the left the attack was stopped cold.
As fast as the Japs came, they were mowed down by automatic rifles and machine guns. The enemy assault gradually

focused on a draw where some American tanks were parked. The tanks fired their 75s at the charging masses. At first the Japs attacked the steel monsters like swarms of ants, firing their rifles at the metal sides and clambering up and over the tanks in a vain attempt to get at the crews inside. They screamed and pounded drunkenly on the turrets and locked hatches, but in their excitement they failed to damage a single tank. Finally, as if engaged in a wild game of follow-the-leader, many of them streamed past the tanks, down the draw toward the beach.

The rest, cringing before the tank fire, moved to the left, hoping to break through our lines and get to the draw farther down the slope of the ridge, behind the tanks. The front they now charged was that of B Company. Here, against the 75 men, the full force of the Japanese attack broke.

In their three-man foxhole, the rifleman Martinez and his two companions had maintained steady fire directly ahead, diverting the first rush of Japs to other sections of the line. During a pause in the fighting, one man left the hole to go back for more hand grenades. Martinez and a Marine named Wimmer were left alone. Around them they saw some of the other Marines withdrawing, sliding down the ridge to a secondary line of foxholes about ten yards to the rear. Here and there, in the light of the flares, they could see them pulling back wounded men.

Trying to decide whether to withdraw themselves, Martinez and Wimmer were confronted suddenly by the first wave of Japs. With bayonets fixed, the enemy came more slowly, throwing grenades and then falling to the ground to wait for the bursts. The first grenades exploded around the Marines without harming them. Then one shattered Wimmer's rifle, and the two men decided it was time to withdraw.

As they crawled out of their foxhole and ran and slid down the slope of the ridge, they noticed a group of screaming figures pour over the crest farther to the right and run headlong down the hill. It was the first indication that the enemy were breaking through. Now Japs would be in our rear, and it would no longer be easy to tell friend from foe.

Martinez and Wimmer reached their platoon command post—an old shellhole ten yards from the top of the ridge, held by Second Lieutenant Edward W. Mulcahy. When the two Marines reached him, Mulcahy was trying desperately to make his field telephone work; but the wires to the rear had already been cut by mortar shells.

Wimmer slid into the hole beside the Lieutenant, and Martinez lay on the forward lip of earth as protection with his rifle. The night was hideous with explosions, lights, screaming enemy, and the odor of *sake*. Against the skyline a handful of Japs appeared. Martinez fired at them, and they backed out of sight. A moment later a string of hand grenades rolled down toward the Marines. Though most of them bounced harmlessly by to explode behind them, one blew up in front of Wimmer's face. Fragments shattered Mulcahy's carbine and struck him on the left side of the head and body. It felt as if he had been slammed with a two-by-four plank.

When he regained his breath, he saw Wimmer holding out his pistol.

"You take it, Lieutenant," Wimmer said in a strange voice.

The Lieutenant protested. The enlisted man would need the weapon for himself.

Wimmer raised his head and smiled. "That's all right, sir," he breathed. "I can't see any more."

The shocked Lieutenant tried to bandage Wimmer's splintered face. The noise from the top of the ridge showed that Marines were still up there, fighting back. It gave the three men hope. The Lieutenant began to shout in the night, like a football coach "Hold that line, men! You can do it!"

The Marine line on the crest, however, had by now disintegrated into a handful of desperate knots of men, fighting together with the fury of human beings trying not to be killed.

Action around two heavy machine guns was typical of what was occurring. A Jap grenade hit one gun, temporarily putting it out of action. The crew members fixed it quickly and started firing again. A second grenade hit the gun's jacket and exploded, knocking off the cover and putting it completely out of the fight. The same blast wounded one of the men. His three companions moved him to a foxhole ten yards behind the shattered gun. One man jumped in beside him, and the other two ran back to the machine-gun foxholes with their carbines. Heaving grenades like wild men, they managed to stall any Jap frontal charge for the moment.

Meanwhile, the other gun was also silenced. Riflemen in foxholes near by heard a sudden unearthly screaming from the gun position. By the wavering light of flares, they saw one of the crew members trying to pull a Japanese bayonet out of another Marine's body. The same instant a wave of Japs appeared from nowhere and swept over both men. Three of the enemy, stopping at the silent machine gun, tried to turn it around to fire at the Marines. In their hysteria, one of them pulled the trigger before the gun was turned, and the bullets sprayed a group of Japs racing across the top of the ridge. Finally the Japs tried to lift the entire gun on its mount and turn the whole thing. A Marine automatic rifleman blasted them with his BAR, and the Japs dropped the gun. Two of them fell over the bodies of the Marine crew. The third pulled out a grenade and, holding it to his head, blew himself up. A moment later another band of Japs appeared. Again, several paused at the gun and tried to swing the heavy weapon around. They had almost succeeded, when from the darkness a lone, drunken Jap raced headlong at them, tripped several feet away over a body, and flew through the air. There was a blinding flash as he literally blew apart. He had been a human bomb, carrying a land mine and a blast charge on his waist.

Other units all along the line had equally serious moments during the night. Though none had been overrun like B Company, several withdrawals occurred. On the left of B Company, however, A Company also stood firm, inspired by Captain William G. Shoemaker, one of the most popular officers in the 3d Division. As wave after wave of Japs rushed A Company's lines, only to be hurled back, Captain Shoemaker made his way calmly among his men, exhorting them to hold.

"If we go, the whole beachhead goes," he explained. "It's up to us to stay here."

Once a rumor swept along the line that the order had been given to withdraw. Men looked around wildly for confirmation. Captain Shoemaker heard the rumor. He leaped to his feet—a hulk of a man, wrapped in a captured Jap trenchcoat—and roared into the night: "By God, we hold here! The beachhead depends on us!"

His men held.

At about 0600, three hours after the enemy attack had begun, a last wave of Japs charged over the top of the hill. It was the wildest, most drunken group of all, bunched together, howling, stumbling and waving swords, bayonets, and long poles. Some were already wounded and were swathed in gory bandages. The Marines yelled back at them and chopped them down in their mad rush. In a moment it was over. The last wave of the three-hour attack died to a man.

But daylight revealed in all their seriousness how successful the earlier charges had been. It was then that the furious, pellmell Jap attacks had begun to hit our rear units.

Immediately behind the punctured 21st Marine line, engineers, artillerymen, and 21st CP personnel formed a secondary line of defense. Other groups, armed with grenades and automatic weapons, moved through the wooded draws and valleys behind our front, in a roving attempt to find the Japs.

The prompt action saved a potentially serious situation. The Jap plan had counted on driving our Marine line straight back into the sea, first piercing it so that the remnants would have to withdraw, and then fanning out in the rear, disrupting our communications and disorganizing the elements on the beach. The attacking enemy, never well organized and from the start under the influence of alcohol, disintegrated once it got through our lines until it became a hodge-podge of wandering bands and individuals without leadership, communications, or well-defined aims. Some of them managed to do damage, like the group that hit our artillery CP. Others caused temporary disruptions, like the mob that stumbled on our Division hospital. But they were only small groups without tactical coördination, and they became easy prey for our mopping-up bands. By noon we had wiped out most of them. The rest of the enemy took to caves to hide and—like bewildered, sick animals—to puzzle over their fate.

As our units re-formed their lines, it was found that Company B had almost been wiped out during the night. Only 18 men remained out of the 75 who had dug in the evening before. The survivors were put into another company, and B Company temporarily ceased to exist.

Many more of our men were killed or wounded that morning mopping up the scattered Jap bands behind our lines. What happened at the artillery CP, where Lieutenant Rodgers and some of our shipboard comrades lost their lives, occurred also around other units. One of our most tragic losses was that of Captain William O'Brien, the 3d Division's Legal Officer, who was liked by everyone who knew him. Although a staff officer, he voluntarily led a squad through the hills above the Division CP looking for Japs. Somehow the other men lost sight of him, and they came back without him. One of his closest friends was our adjutant, Major Bob Kriendler, who had been busy keeping tabs on our casualties as they piled up during the night. It had been a sad job for him, for many of the dead and wounded had been his friends. Then someone came in to say that Bill O'Brien was missing. Major Kriendler couldn't believe that anything had happened to the Legal Officer. He kept his fingers crossed and assured everyone that his friend would turn up during the day. But just after noon, a man came into Kriendler's tent on some other business. "Say, it's too bad about Bill O'Brien, isn't it?" he said to the Major.

Kriendler thought the newcomer was merely repeating the rumor. "He'll turn up," he replied.

But the newcomer leaned forward. "I don't think you understand," he went on. "I just saw Bill down at the cemetery—they brought him in. No one saw him get killed. They just found his body."

The banzai charge on Guam was never fully reported by the civilian press. Most of the civilian correspondents at the time were on the other beachhead with the 1st Brigade and the Army. In front of our lines our bulldozers and burial squads found some eight hundred Japs. Behind our lines we killed or sealed in caves about two thousand more. The newspapers in the United States put it simply: an enemy counter-attack was repulsed with severe losses to the Japanese. Such reporting could not convey the terror of the night attack or the businesslike devotion to duty of our men. Because the eighteen survivors of B Company and the others who stood all along the line that night failed to give way, the beachhead was saved, as Captain Shoemaker had said it would be. By maintaining their line, our men were able to close the gaps, trap the enemy in the rear, and the following day launch a new attack of their own.

The Jap charge had wasted the cream of the enemy troops on the island. After the failure of the charge they had nothing more to oppose us with. They continued to hurl smaller attacks against us at night—some of them drunken assaults—and retreat before us by day; but their offensive power was broken.

As we pushed inland, some of our units continued to have desperate moments among the wooded hills and valleys. In many places the hills were steep coral formations that afforded the Japs numerous caves in which to hide. Many of these caves were neutralized by "Slug" Marvin's flame-throwing team. Once a company commander sent for Marvin and told him that he had seen a Jap duck into a cave. He asked Marvin to get him to surrender or seal him up. So Marvin climbed on top of the cave and hollered: "Nipponese, take off your clothes, come out with your hands up, and we'll take you prisoner and treat you well."

Instead of one voice replying from inside the cave, several called back: "Go to hell!"

Marvin then threw in three thermite grenades and listened. When the hiss of the grenades quieted, he still heard jabbering inside. He ordered a flame-thrower used. A thirty-foot stream of fire flashed into the cave and licked the walls and floor. The jabbering continued.

"TNT!" Marvin yelled.

They threw in twenty-five-pound TNT charges, used the flame-throwers again, and then sprayed the inside with an automatic rifle. At last everything was still. Marvin pushed impatiently into the cave's mouth. Inside he counted thirty dead Japs. Later, when rear elements came up and made a thorough check of the cave, they found sixty-three dead enemy. The cave, which the company commander had seen *one* Jap enter, was big enough to hold five hundred men at a time!

Marvin's team eventually got worn out. Of twenty-one men who had landed with him, only six were left on their feet. Marvin sent the survivors back for a rest and volunteered to take over a rifle platoon whose commanding officer had been a casualty. Leading the platoon forward one day, "Slug," in his usual fashion, got far out ahead.

He turned and yelled back. "Come on up here, you men! I'm not a scout!"

Just then something hit his cartridge belt: a Jap hand grenade, a rifle shot—no one ever knew. "Slug's" ammunition exploded into him and around him like a fireworks display. Litter bearers carried him back to the beach, and he died a few days later on a ship. He was awarded the Navy Cross posthumously.

Close-range fighting and sudden death from small arms and occasional artillery shells characterized the remainder of the battle for Guam. By D plus 8, we seemed to be well in control of the situation, although we were still suffering casualties. Our Division line swung around, joined the Brigade and the 77th Division who had pushed inland from the other beachhead, and established a line of attack clear across the island. Then we moved abreast, heading for the northern coast of Guam.

About this time, I left Wheaton and went to the 9th Marines, whose three combat correspondents had all been casualties on D-day. The 9th Marines were pushing the attack in the center of our line and meeting little resistance. We entered Agana, the capital city of Guam, and found nothing there. The town in which our men had looked forward to having their first liberty in a year was a complete shambles and deserted. The Japs did not choose to defend it, possibly because by then their communications and command were thoroughly disrupted. It would have made an excellent site for defense, however. Our naval and aerial shelling had turned it into a jungle of ruins.

Moving quickly, we left Agana and occupied the Japanese Tiyan airfield on the other side of town. The field looked like a country airport back home, though not so good. A few scattered buildings had been smashed to ruins. About twenty-five shattered Jap planes lay in the bushes and among trees along the strip. The area was deserted, and we pushed on, entering the jungle of the northern half of Guam.

It was impossible to see more than a few feet ahead through the thick foliage. We moved in skirmish lines but knew that we were leaving enemy stragglers behind. They were cut off and leaderless and were mostly wandering around in the jungle trying to stay out of our sight. They hid in caves during the day and came out to try to find other Japs at night.

We were leaving them to rear elements for mopping up. Our commanding officers wanted the rifle units to keep going and wipe out any large band of Japs they found, so that no sizeable enemy group could get its breath and reorganize.

What happened when the Japs got a chance to reorganize was made grimly evident to us soon after we passed the Tiyan airfield. We had emerged on a narrow jungle road, leading to a village called Finegayan. It was about noon, and I was helping to guide a member of an artillery forward observing team up to our front-line company. A radioman, he was relieving someone who had been with us five days. The FO team members each worked five days with the forward companies, then rested in reserve a couple of days.

Along the road Jap snipers took potshots at us. We clung to the side of the trail beneath the protection of tall grass and bushes. We passed many Jap bodies, lying on the road and in the brush. They had just been killed, their skin was loose and wrinkled, and the blood was still red on their clothes.

We noticed an unusual amount of firing ahead of us. Rifle and machine-gun shots cracked through the grass. Mortar shells crashed among the trees, sending up columns of black smoke. Overhead one of our observation planes was whirring back and forth. Going on, we reached a green wooden house by the side of the road. About thirty Marines lay on stretchers in front—it was an aid station. Doctors and corpsmen were working over a line of men. Two jeep ambulances were being filled with wounded. It looked like the biggest battle since we had left the ridges above the beachhead.

We found the company CP to which the radioman had been ordered to report. The Marines were crouched in shell-holes and newly dug foxholes. The dirt—red and moist, almost like mud—covered the men's clothes and faces and hands. We were ordered to get down and stay down. The firing ahead was sharp. Bullets were striking trees around us. Men scurried back and forth through the grass, hunched over, the way they had moved along the beach on D-day.

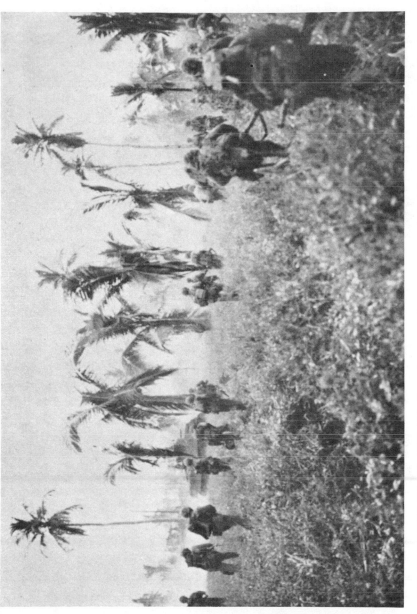

NEAR FINEGAYAN, GUAM. Our men spread out, as a group of re-formed Japs try to ambush us.

AMBUSHED. Our men take cover in the boondocks until Jap mortar and riflemen can be located.

"This war ain't over yet," a sergeant said, chewing on a wad of tobacco. "I guess you know they got a lot of our guys here just now." He waved his arm around at the grass. "We got over a hundred Nips in the past half-hour, I reckon."

Although the sounds of battle were all around us, we couldn't see anything. After some time we could reconstruct what had happened. It had been an enemy ambush. The Japs had had two road blocks in parallel lines across the road, about a hundred yards apart. There were mines in the roads, then antitank and heavier guns on both sides of the road, and, stretching inland, round spider pits dug into the ground to keep the tanks from going around the traps. The pits had been filled with Japs ordered to halt the tanks.

Somehow the tanks got through, but the infantry didn't. The first row of Japs let most of our men through, then opened fire on their backs. At the same moment the second row of Japs opened fire on our men's faces. The rear line of Japs were eliminated in bloody, hand-to-hand fighting. Some of the Japs jumped out of their pits to run. Our men cut them down. One Marine, PFC Francis P. Witek, killed fourteen Japs with his BAR, fearlessly standing up in the open to get a good aim at them. Then he was killed by a Jap hand grenade. (Witek received the Congressional Medal of Honor posthumously for this gallantry.)

The battle ended almost as suddenly as it had begun. A short time after the radioman and I arrived, the firing slackened and then ceased. Men lifted themselves warily and poked around in the grass. We went forward along the road about fifty yards and saw the road block that had trapped our men. A Jap 77, with big wooden wheels, stood silently against the trunk of a breadfruit tree; around it sprawled dead Japs. In from the road was a line of spider pits—round holes about two feet across and three feet deep. In each one there were two dead Japs, mashed and gory. Some had been hit with grenades, others looked as if tanks had run over them. Around the lips of their holes lay unused ammunition, black and red hand grenades, and Molotov cocktails—green *sake* bottles filled with gasoline. None of the bottles had been used. Some of our men poked for souvenirs, using their bayonets to cut the belts and buttons of the dead Japs so as to see whether they were wearing flags underneath their clothes. One Jap had a battle flag wrapped around his leg beneath a puttee. The white of the flag was covered with characters in black ink—good-luck messages from his friends and family back home. One of our interpreters, glancing at the flag, pointed to one set of characters. "That," he said, "reads: 'Death to the Anglo-American devils.'"

The man who had gotten the flag grinned. "Now ain't that sweet?" he muttered.

The road was open now, and I left the radioman and went back to the aid station. Somebody there said we had killed one hundred and nine Japs and had had almost as many casualties ourselves. Stretcher bearers were still looking around through the tall grass for our dead. A jeep came up, pulling a trailer full of new shoes and dungarees.

"Them's for my boys," the driver shouted gleefully. "I never forget them. Tonight I'm bringing up hot soup and doughnuts!"

He unhitched the trailer and took me back in the jeep. The smell along the road was growing stronger. The dead were turning ivory-colored. We passed a Marine lying on his back just off the road.

"Keep low," the driver said. "A sniper just winged that poor guy while I was coming up."

We got back without incident, and I returned to the Division CP. Some of the civilian correspondents were there. They had brought mimeographed copies of the day's news from one of the transports off shore—news that had been picked up by radio from San Francisco. One of the items said that the battle of Guam was almost over. I felt a little bitter when I went to bed that night.

The next day Captain Shoemaker of A Company, the 21st

Marines—the officer who had gallantly exhorted.his men to hold the line on the ridge the night of the banzai charge—was killed. Ironically, he was doing nothing at the time but resting. His men were taking a breather, lying along both sides of the same road on which we had been ambushed. Suddenly an enemy 77 shell swooshed through the air from somewhere up north and crashed with a burst of smoke. Fragments ripped into the Captain, and he died almost immediately. The men gathered around his body while they waited for a jeep ambulance, and many of them cried. One man with tears staining his dusty face turned away. "All the good ones go," he said.

On the 11th of August—D plus 20—we reached the cliffs along the northern shore of Guam and looked down at the surf breaking on the reef six hundred feet below. We sent patrols down the cliffside and out to the breakers. Then we announced that Guam had been secured.

That night I went back to the Division CP that had been moved into the jungle about halfway up the island. We had set up a fly tent and slept on top of the ground beneath the canvas. In the middle of the night somebody in a foxhole on one side of us began shooting—past us. Someone on the other side returned the fire. Others joined in, and the bullets flew back and forth. Suddenly a grenade hissed through the night and exploded. The fragments rattled against our fly tent. We pressed ourselves as flat against the ground as we could, praying that nothing would hit us. Suddenly in the darkness one of the other men in our tent yelled out: "God damn it, don't you know this rock is secured!"

It would be a nice ending to the story to say that this stopped the senseless firing around us, but it didn't. And it would also be nice to say that the island at that time was *really* secured, but it wasn't. There was still a lot of fighting on Guam ahead of us.

V

The Chamorros

WHEN we had first left the beaches and begun to move inland, we had come on the people of Guam—the native Chamorros. We encountered them in small groups, here and there, as they emerged from caves and broke free from Jap concentration camps. There was never any question of their loyalty to us: They were hysterically glad to see us. They burned with a desire for revenge on the Japs who had oppressed them for two and a half years. They wanted to join us, to borrow weapons from us and help us regain the island. When Guam was announced secured, we found that we welcomed their assistance. There were many thousands of by-passed Japs still on the island, hiding in remote parts of the jungles and cave sections. The Guamanians knew these areas better than we did. We gave them weapons and enlisted them on our side in an unpublicized guerrilla-type battle that was to last many months.

The 23,000 Guamanian people were a peace-loving race of mixed Spanish and Polynesian blood. The men were husky and good-looking; the women, erect and of athletic bearing, with long black hair that fell attractively around their shoulders. In the old Spanish days Guam had been a principal stop for galleons plying between Mexico and the Philippine Islands, and the Guamanian people had absorbed much from

both places. They sang Mexican folksongs and sent their
children to school at Manila. To a considerable extent both
the people and the countryside reminded one of Mexico.

After the Spanish-American War, Guam became an American possession. Under our tutelage the people learned the
ways of democracy, while modern schools, sanitation, and public works gradually raised their standards of culture and well-
being. Coincidently the Guamanians mingled with and married American sailors and Marines stationed on Guam, and
soon the island became an outpost of the American way of
life. The Gonzalezes and the Benaventes and the other people
of the island became Hollywood fans; they played baseball
and had drugstores that served sodas and sundaes; they
collected swing records of the best United States bands; they
enlisted in the United States Navy and they sent their
daughters to convents in the United States. The wealthier
families took long vacations in the States, visiting the National
Parks and the Capital and wondering if and when Guam
would become a State and have its own representatives in
Congress. On the island they had a little self-government:
they elected a Congress of their own that served under an
American-appointed Governor, the people being "nationals,"
not citizens. They farmed, raised cattle, and engaged in
business in Agana and the small towns. Many of them worked
for the Navy. There were Guamanian stenographers in the
offices and Guamanian trained nurses in the hospital. They
had their own militia, trained by the Marines, for defense.

The Japs came on December 8, 1941. They bombed the
Marine and Navy installations for a couple of days. Then invasion forces landed early one morning. There was a brief
running fight. The Guamanian militia fought side by side
with the Marines. There were some deaths before the handful of defenders were overwhelmed in the plaza before the
Governor's Palace in Agana. The Japs arrested all Americans
and persons suspected of being too zealously pro-American.
Some escaped to the hills and hid in caves. All except one

—Radioman First Class George Ray Tweed of the U. S. Navy —were eventually captured or killed.

The Japs called the people together and told them that the war would soon be over. The American fleet, they said, was sunk, the American forces were dispersed. Japan's aim, the invaders announced, was to include Guam in the new "Greater East Asia Co-Prosperity Sphere." All the people had to do was "coöperate" with the new government. Then there would be peace, prosperity, and happiness for everyone on the island.

A short time later most of Japan's military forces left the island, and Guam was placed under a civil government. The war was going well for the Japs, and Guam was too far in their rear to worry about. Then the Kohatsu Company came in— a private exploitation outfit, subsidiary of one of the big business monopolies in Japan. Guam and its people were handed over to the Kohatsu Company—lock, stock, and barrel —in return, of course, for taxes. The Kohatsu development group brought in its own police and doctor. All food and merchandise of every kind imported into Guam was brought in by Kohatsu and sold to the people at whatever the monopoly felt like charging. The rice paddies and farms of Guam produced for Kohatsu, which set its own rates of payment. New labor regulations went into effect. Women were ordered into the fields to work for a few cents a day or a handful of rice; the Kohatsu's policemen stood about and struck them if they didn't work hard enough. The native men worked on roads and the airfields.

For a time the Japs were not too strict. There were punishments, often more childish than stern, though occasionally an offender had his head chopped off. But the Japs continued to make efforts to win the people over to "coöperation." Eventually, however, the war turned against Japan, and the United States began to move back towards Guam. Jap troops returned to the island to build defenses. Secret police and Navy terror societies began to operate. Hunts were instigated for pro-Americans. There were many arrests and executions, and eventually a reign of terror broke out on the island. Our fliers began to bomb Guam, and our fleet closed in to shell the Jap positions. An increasing number of Guamanians were accused of trying to aid us and of secretly working for our return. Finally, just before our invasion, the whole civil population was ordered to leave its homes and march into concentration camps in the hills. Some got away from the police and hid in caves; others were caught trying to escape and were shot or bayoneted to death. On the day we landed on Guam there were no civilians in sight. They were huddled in misery in the camps in the hills, where they had been for more than a month. There in the mud, dying of disease and starvation, we were eventually to find them.

During our first days on the island, however, we hadn't known any of this, and we wondered where all the people were. Some of our sailors, who were Guamanians and who had landed with us, looked forlornly at the wreckage of farms and homes of people they had known. One boy saw his own home—the house in which he had been born—a pile of splintered wood and crushed stone. "My people can't be alive," he said. "I can only hope."

Later he found them in one of the camps. His mother had died there. His father and his three sisters—all in the first stages of tuberculosis—embraced him proudly. They hadn't seen or heard of him since before December 1941.

"We knew you would come back," they said. "It is what kept us alive."

The first contact we had with civilians came soon after we widened our perimeter to include the outskirts of the battered city of Agana. One day a radio message came back from one of our outposts: "Twenty women, several babies, one cow, and a sewing machine coming through our lines."

More groups followed—old, gnarled men with sticks; crones with wispy white hair, lace dresses, and no shoes; young girls in mud-stained rags, carrying naked babies; little boys and girls holding onto each other's hands fearfully. Coming out of hiding places near the shore, they told us they had seen us land and had waited for us to come near enough for them to emerge and enter our lines. One woman had a tiny American flag that she had made on her sewing machine in a cave; it had seven red and white stripes and a field of blue, and was fashioned from a dress. She had waved it at our ships from her cave, hoping to be rescued, but none of our vessels had seen her.

The first liberated Chamorros were housed in tents in two camps—one near our Division CP and the other on a hill overlooking the Brigade's beachhead. Marine Major General Henry L. Larsen had landed on that beachhead to take over the island at the earliest moment as Island Commander. His first job was to care for the civilian refugees. The biggest problem seemed to be the babies, of whom there were many. Like the adults, most of them were suffering from malnutrition, and from dysentery and other illnesses, and were covered with jungle sores. At first we had no baby specialists with us, so our Navy corpsmen had to do what they could. As the corpsmen, in turn, were puzzled over where to find the supplies they needed, the problem created confusion around our Division CP. Day and night we heard babies crying as we went about the work of battle or lay in our foxholes listening for Japs. Our Quartermaster, a grizzled old Regular, was called on for nipples, safety pins, and diapers. He could only scratch his head, examine boxes of helmets, mosquito netting, and mess gear, and suggest that the corpsmen see General Larsen on the other beachhead.

One of the first of the freed Chamorros was a former member of the Guam Congress, a fifty-year-old man named Gaily R. Kamminga, who had snow-white hair and wrinkled brown skin. He was greeted by some of the Navy officers who had landed with us and who had previously served on Guam and remembered Kamminga. Kamminga came into our

HOME WAS NEVER LIKE THIS. Night after night, in the northern boon-docks of Guam, we lived in holes, on guard against straggling Japs.

SOME JAPS SURRENDER. Adamson and Henderson in our LCI's dinghy take a Jap straggler off the Guam reef.

camp on a truck from the front lines where a roadside patrol had found him. He was carrying a little pillow with him. After he shook hands with his old friends, he suddenly ripped open the pillow.

"Look," he said proudly. "I have saved this all through the enemy occupation."

Carefully, he pulled out a faded American flag.

"This is the flag," he said, "that flew over the Piti Navy Yard on the day the Japanese invaded us. I took it and sewed it into this pillow. The Japanese never found it. When they moved my niece and me to the penal camp last February, they gave me permission to take along one article for my comfort. I chose this pillow."

Kamminga, who was of mixed Dutch and Chamorran ancestry, told us that the Japanese had watched him closely during the period of occupation because he had previously been a member of the American-sponsored island Congress, and he had been one of the first men ordered into the concentration camps.

"The Japanese," he said, "are very much afraid of those who might be pro-American. In one town they caught a little boy watching a dogfight between Japanese and American planes. They said the boy was hoping the American would win because his brother was in the United States Navy. The boy made no reply, so they put him in the public square and chopped his head off."

One man who came into our lines at this time, José B. Acfarre, forty-two years old, who had formerly worked at the American naval hospital in Agana, was still shaking from his experiences.

"The other night," he related, "the Japanese came through the concentration camp and selected twenty-nine of us who they said were secretly wishing for American victory. They herded us into a cave and threw hand grenades in on us. Those in front were killed, but some of us at the back were only slightly hurt. After the Japanese left, five of us who were still alive escaped into the woods. We wandered for several days. One of our men was caught by a Jap patrol and bayoneted to death. The rest of us finally went over a hill and straight into the American lines."

Since all the refugees told us of misery and danger existing at the concentration camps, we tried to reach the camps and liberate the people as quickly as possible. The Guamanians themselves, however, beat us to it. At one camp they finally overran the Jap guards, killed some and drove the others away, then waited for our forces to appear. At the other camps the Japs, realizing we were coming closer, just took their equipment and weapons and disappeared, leaving the people free.

One of the largest camps, a big clearing in the jungle near a place called Yona, was first reached by the 77th Division. Here thousands of Guamanians were living like savages. Among the trees they had built miserable lean-tos and thatched huts, and crowded together on the mud banks on both sides of a brackish stream. The camp was filled with disease. The Japs had given the people no medical assistance and little food. As the struggle to stay alive had grown harder, sanitary conditions had deteriorated. The minimum of clothing which they had been allowed to take with them had worn out and become torn and dirty. By the time our troops reached the camp, most of the people were in rags. They were weak and coughing and ridden with malnutrition, dysentery, and tuberculosis.

Yet when the Guamanians saw our men arrive, they hobbled to their feet and, holding onto each other, cried and cheered. Many of the youths began to sing the *Marine Hymn*, which they remembered, and an underground, anti-Japanese song that an anonymous Chamorran had written during the enemy occupation. This was the day for which that song had been composed, and the Guamanians sang its crude but meaningful words again and again:

"Early Monday morning
The action came to Guam,
Eighth of December,
Nineteen forty-one.
    Oh, Mr. Sam, Sam, my dear Uncle Sam,
    I want you please come back to Guam.

"Our lives are in danger—
You better come
And kill all the Japanese
Right here on Guam.
    Oh, Mr. Sam, etc.

"We don't like the *sake*,
We like Canadian [whiskey],
We don't like the Japanese—
It's better American.
    Oh, Mr. Sam, etc.

"So long with corned beef,
With bacon and ham,
So long with sandwiches,
With juices and jam.
    Oh, Mr. Sam, etc."

And on and on. During the occupation, the people later told us, the Japs had bribed the Chamorran children with candy to sing *Uncle Sam*. When the children did so, the Jap police took their addresses and went to their homes to arrest their parents as "American sympathizers."

In the center of the compound we found a thatched hut larger than the others. The men had built it as a sort of hospital. Presiding over it was one of the underground heroes of the occupation, a small, kindly doctor named Ramon M. Sablan. The moment the Jap guards fled, he had set up the dispensary and had enlisted the aid of girls in the camp who had previously been nurses at the Navy hospital. Now he was treating some 650 people a day for everything from skin rashes to pneumonia.

Dr. Sablan was forty-two years old. He had studied in the United States for twelve years, being graduated from Oklahoma A & M College and receiving degrees from Missouri State University and the Louisville University Medical School in Kentucky. In 1940 he had returned to Guam to practice medicine. As the Pan American Air Lines doctor at the clipper base, he had met and become friendly with many distinguished passengers flying through. His interests were wide; he liked to discuss economic affairs and the international situation. In November 1941, fearing the outbreak of war with Japan, he had sent his wife and daughter back to the United States. His wife later became a war worker in the Vultee Aircraft Plant in Louisville.

When the Japs came to Guam, all the American doctors were arrested, and Dr. Sablan was prohibited from practicing medicine. To care for the island's thousands of people, the Japs brought in three of their own doctors—two Navy physicians and an employee of the Kohatsu firm.

Within a short time, Chamorros came secretly to Dr. Sablan, complaining that there were not enough Japanese doctors to take care of the civilian population. Dr. Sablan— just as secretly—procured a supply of drugs from the old American drugstore in Agana. Then, traveling covertly at night by foot, bicycle, or carabao-drawn cart, he visited his people.

Several times the Japanese learned of his trips. When they questioned him about them, he explained that they were merely visits to friends. Over a period of two years on these "visits," he delivered more than 150 babies and, working by candlelight with the assistance of farmers and housewives, performed delicate operations that saved the lives of scores of Guamanians.

After the people were driven into the concentration camps, Dr. Sablan again ministered secretly to some of the sick inmates. By this time, however, his supply of drugs was practically exhausted. And the terrible need rose every day.

Hundreds of cases of pneumonia, dysentery, malnutrition, jungle sores, and tuberculosis broke out. And babies were still being born.

Dr. Sablan, with tired eyes and prematurely graying hair, took us around the camp, showing us the problems with which he had tried to cope.

"This teaches us," he said sadly, "how quickly man can degenerate into the state of the animal. These people are used to the same civilization as you are. Now they live like savages, eating and lying in the mud, among the flies from their uncovered excrement." He added bitterly: "This is what the Japanese Greater East Asia Co-Prosperity Sphere has brought us to."

We went into one of the thatched huts, so small that we had to stoop. On the mud floor sat several persons, barefoot, their clothes in tatters. The smell was horrible. The doctor introduced us. The responses were gruntlike sounds. One man stood up uncertainly and bowed. A wrinkled old woman stared up without saying anything. The doctor turned to a stoutish girl of about eighteen, dressed in what looked like a burlap bag. Her hair hung over her brow and head like a mass of black ropes.

"This is Helen," he said. "Helen, have you got that picture you showed me yesterday?"

She nodded.

"Bring it outside in the light."

She followed us hesitantly out of the hut. She seemed shy, almost afraid of us. She held out a snapshot: a well-dressed family posed among the skyscrapers of Radio City, New York.

"That's Helen and her family—a few years ago," Dr. Sablan said. "Do you see what I mean?"

Another Guamanian who was helping to care for his people was the sole surviving native priest, young Father Oscar Calvo. The other island priest, Father Jesus Duenas, was no longer with them, having been killed. The most respected figure on the island during the Jap occupation, he was Guam's outstanding martyr to the cause of freedom, a companion to the many thousands of heroes all over the world who died fighting the Axis countries for religious liberty. He was thirty years old when he was killed. He was the son of a farmer and had attended American grade school in Agana. He had studied under American Jesuit Fathers in Manila and in 1938 had returned to Guam to be ordained to the priesthood by Bishop Miguel Angel Olano of Agana.

When the Japanese came to Guam, they arrested Bishop Olano and ordered Father Duenas to take down all the crosses and religious symbols in the Agana churches. The young priest refused. When the Japs themselves went ahead and did it, Father Duenas left Agana to preach in a small church in Inarajan, his home town across the island. Though the Japs were angry with him, they were so anxious at that time to appease the people of the island and win them over to "coöperation" that they decided to let him alone; they realized that, though young, he was popular with the Guamanians. However, they took Bishop Olano to Japan as a prisoner and sent two Japanese Catholic priests (one of whom was a Monsignor) to the island. The latter tried to win over Father Duenas to the side of the invaders. They talked to the younger native priest, Father Calvo, and asked him to persuade Father Duenas that all would be well if he would coöperate with the Japanese.

Father Duenas's reply was simple: He served only Christ, he said. As long as the Japanese interfered with the religious freedom of his people, he would oppose them.

Several months after the Japanese landed, a letter came from Bishop Olano in Tokyo, naming Father Duenas Pro-Vicar Apostolic of Guam. As the Bishop's vicar, Father Duenas was to continue ministering to the spiritual wants of his people. Dividing the island with Father Calvo, he took the southern half around his home at Inarajan and conducted services again.

The Japanese did not protest. But they did make the priest uncomfortable. They "suggested" that he submit his sermons to a censor. They asked him to make official announcements during the services. And they had spies go to confession to see what he said and how he behaved.

Father Duenas replied by omitting sermons from his services. He refused to read any announcements other than routine notices of meetings and new regulations. And spies he did not fear. His work was the work of Christ only, as he said, and the spies had nothing to report.

Once a month he and Father Calvo met at Agana with the *Minseibu*, which was composed of the Japanese civil Governor and his staff, to discuss the welfare of the people of the island. At each session Father Duenas suggested improvements: The people needed more food and new clothing. The prices set by the Kohatsu Company were too high. The people were being terrorized, treated like slaves. Women, forced to work long hours in the rice fields, were slapped across the face and beaten. There was inadequate medical care.

Each time the Governor promised to look into these matters, and each time he did nothing. Finally Father Duenas spoke up. He told the Governor that nothing ever came of his suggestions, because (as he put it), the Japanese didn't want anything to come of them. The Governor was angered, and the monthly meetings ended.

As admiration for Father Duenas's courage spread among the people, his standing with the Japanese went down. The *Kempeitai* (Jap secret police) ordered a Chamorro named Felipe Camacho Mendiola, from the nearby island of Rota, to spy on the priest. Mendiola made it known that Father Duenas was suspected of being pro-American and of working secretly for the return of the Americans to Guam. A more serious charge was that the priest was believed to be in communication with Radioman Tweed, who was hiding somewhere on the island. Tweed was suspected by the Japanese of having a radio set and being in touch with the United

States Navy. Occasionally, when an American submarine would slip into Apra Harbor and sink a Jap ship, Tweed was thought to be responsible. The angered Japs would take up their manhunt again, and everyone suspected of knowing Tweed's whereabouts would be rounded up, tortured and, when failing to give information, killed.

According to the Rota spy, Father Duenas was believed by the Japs to know where Tweed was hiding. Efforts were made to have the priest show his hand in such a way that the people could not complain if the Japanese arrested him. Friends, neighbors, even Father Calvo, were asked to suggest to Father Duenas that he "coöperate." Father Duenas refused to listen to them.

One day, when Father Duenas was absent from his home parish, the two Japanese priests on the island paid an unannounced visit to Inarajan and conducted services in Father Duenas's church. In their sermons they hinted to the people that Father Duenas was hostile to the Japanese. They went on to say that the American forces were beaten and would never return, that the Japanese wanted only peace for the people of the island, and that, when everyone coöperated, there would be great prosperity and happiness.

When Father Duenas returned to Inarajan and heard what had occurred, he was roused to white heat. He sat down and wrote to the Japanese priests, telling them that his people did not believe they were Catholic priests, but Japanese spies. He quoted the late Pope Benedict XV, who during the First World War had said that it was not proper for a priest in a foreign country to preach of his own country's greatness.

What the Japanese priests did with the letter was not known. Soon afterwards Father Duenas was called to the office of the *Minseibu* and questioned. The interrogation was brief and polite. When asked about his loyalty to Japan, the priest gave his usual answer: he was concerned only with the religious freedom of his people. The Japanese released him and he returned to his parish.

HE GAVE UP. *Sick, hungry, afraid that we will kill him, a Jap straggler surrenders to our LCI.*

RESULTS OF OUR MOPPING-UP. Jap civilians who had hidden in the Guam jungle surrender at the southern shore of the island

At that time there lived in Inarajan a woman of about forty named Nettie Durham, the daughter of a Chamorro woman and an ex-United States Marine. She had been married twice, both times to American sailors. Her second husband, Thomas Durham, was taken prisoner when the Japanese landed on Guam and was sent to Japan. Nettie stayed behind and eventually became friendly with a petty Japanese official named Churima.

Churima, who was younger than Nettie, was an assistant in the *Minseibu* office in Inarajan. Gradually, it was whispered about (according to the Guamanians who recounted Father Duenas's story to us) that it was really Nettie who was running the *Minseibu* office in that district. Everything she wanted, Churima had done for her. She was installed in a big house and lived (according to the people of the district) like an aristocrat.

Complaints about Nettie reached Father Duenas. He heard that, through Churima, local men were being forced to work for Nettie, that farmers' chickens and produce were requisitioned for her table, and that, when the people protested, the Japanese threatened them with arrest.

During a trip to Agana, Father Duenas stopped at the main office of the *Minseibu* and discussed the people's complaints about Nettie and Churima. One of Churima's friends was in the office and overheard him. When the priest left, the friend 'phoned Churima and told him Father Duenas had reported him to the high Jap officials.

Nettie was irate over what she considered interference by the priest and, with Churima, she plotted to destroy him. Hiring a local farmer named Pio Naputi, who was a member of Father Duenas's parish but who had been convinced that Japan would win the war, she promised him a position of power if he would furnish evidence that would send the priest to jail.

At about the same time, Father Duenas became involved in a personal quarrel with Churima's superior in the Inarajan

Minseibu. The Jap official had previously "borrowed" the priest's saddle; now he refused to return it. Father Duenas asked the *Kempeitai* to help him to get it back. Instead of doing anything about it, the *Kempeitai* officials informed the *Minseibu* representative that the priest had complained about him. The *Minseibu* official smarted with anger, and he was still smarting when Churima appeared one morning at his office with the farmer-informer Pio Naputi. Naputi had something to "tell on" Father Duenas. The *Minseibu* officials listened eagerly as the farmer reported a brief tale that he hoped would make him a person of importance under the Japs. Someone had told him, he said, that once Father Duenas had stated publicly that he had fed an American sailor (Tweed).

It was what the Japanese wanted. On July 2, 1944, nineteen days before D-day on Guam, an unarmed Chamorro interpreter, working for the Inarajan *Minseibu*, went to Father Duenas's home and in a polite and oily voice told him that the *Minseibu* would "appreciate" his reporting at its local office. Father Duenas accompanied the interpreter. He was used to such requests. At the office this time, however, he found his nephew, Edward Duenas, a 31-year-old island attorney, who had received a similar summons.

In front of the interpreter (who later was one of the persons who corroborated the details of the story), both men were questioned about Tweed. To all questions concerning the seaman, the priest replied: "That is for me to know and you to find out." The Japanese became impatient. Pio Naputi was summoned. He repeated his story before the priest. Father Duenas replied that Naputi was not telling the truth.

The Japs now turned to their last recourse: Father Duenas and his nephew were slapped, punched, and beaten. When they fell, they were kicked and whipped with wire lashes until they bled from a score of wounds. Edward Duenas finally cried out that his uncle did know Tweed. The priest, however, accused the Japs of torturing his nephew so that he no longer knew what he was saying.

After midnight the *Minseibu* turned the two almost un-conscious men over to the secret police. They were put in an army truck and driven across Guam to Agana. After further torture they were placed in a concentration camp at the near-by town of Sinajana, then transferred to a remote camp at Tae, belonging to the *Kaigontai*, a food supply branch of the Japanese Navy. They were questioned again concerning Tweed's whereabouts. When Father Duenas remained silent, he was ordered executed.

"I have no fear of death," he murmured to his captors.

At four in the morning the priest and his nephew were taken from the thatched huts in which they had been kept. Their wrists tied behind their backs, they were forced to kneel and bow their heads. Before the eyes of two civilian witnesses (both Chamorro interpreters from Saipan), the executioner brought his long sword down. But he did a bad job: it took several strokes to sever each man's head. In the early dawn—to the thunder of American warships which even then were heralding the return of liberty to Guam—the young priest and his nephew were buried in an unmarked pit. Months later Marines helped to find the grave and give the martyrs a decent burial.

None of the Guamanians who told us the facts about Father Duenas seemed to know whether the priest had actually fed Tweed. Certainly scores of Chamorros took care of the American sailor during his months of hiding, and many died for him beneath the Japanese long sword. In later months, while we were on Guam, the Chamorros with whom we became friendly sat in our tents and talked about Tweed and told us that they hoped that he appreciated the sacrifices they had made for him. They didn't think he liked them, but they protected him because to them he was a symbol of America and the Americans' return; as long as he was still alive, they had a link with the United States. The men of our Division never saw Tweed, though we heard a lot about him from the Guamanians. As soon as they were freed they asked us:

"Where is Tweed? Did he escape?" Tweed did escape. He flashed a signal from the shore to an American warship, and a small boat came in and got him. He had no opportunity to thank the Chamorros and say goodbye, because by that time they were all in concentration camps.

Soon after the camp at Yona was freed, General Larsen's organization went to work to rehabilitate the people. Navy doctors and corpsmen helped Dr. Sablan clean up the camp and bring the health situation under control. Captured Jap stores and American rations were distributed. And one Sunday, with Father Calvo officiating, there was a Thanksgiving Mass.

On this occasion some of our men were drawn around the camp with rifles and machine guns to guard against interference from Jap stragglers. In the center of the camp an American flag was raised, and several hundred schoolchildren sang patriotic American songs. Few of them could speak English, for under the Japs our language had been banned; the old people had gone back to Spanish, the midde-aged to Chamorran, and the schoolchildren had learned Japanese. But, somehow, parents had taught their children the English words of *God Bless America* and *America, the Beautiful*, and they sang them now for their first flag-raising in beautiful, high, liquid voices.

After the Mass some news photographers appeared to take pictures of the people. The young barefoot girls saw them and scampered into their huts. A few moments later they reappeared with their long tresses combed and filled with flowers and ribbons. One photographer turned to a Guamanian man. "What's the idea?" he asked. "We came to take pictures of refugees, and they doll themselves up." The Guamanian grinned. "They think some movie scout may see the pictures," he said. "They all want to go to Hollywood."

As we moved north through the jungle, we liberated other

camps and set more of the island people free. All of them were in the same state of hunger and wretchedness, and all greeted us with the same enthusiasm. At one camp First Lieutenant George B. Hinde met his old Spanish professor from Ohio State University, a Guamanian named José Palomo; it was a joyful reunion for both men.

Through the freed people and the stories they told us of their suffering under the Japs, we added to our knowledge of the enemy and his system. We found also that, despite the terror that had been on Guam, the Japanese had had a hard time trying to implant their propaganda among the Chamorros because the latter had been used to the truth and free expression. They looked with contempt on the Japs, who seemed to believe what they were preaching. Soon after Guam was seized, Japanese soldiers repeated to some of the people what they themselves had been told: that Washington, D.C., had been captured and that President Roosevelt had gone crazy and was riding a bicycle around the cellar of the White House. The Guamanians, realizing that the Japs believed this, laughed behind their hands at their simple-minded conquerors. Later, a contingent of Jap troops arriving on the island showed the people pictures of themselves in furry caps and earmuffs and mounted on shaggy ponies. The photographs had been taken in Manchuria, but the Japs alleged that they were taken in California, where they said they had just been. Again the people had to hide their laughter.

Many of the Guamanians also ridiculed the technical backwardness of the Japs. Chamorro boys who had had mechanical training under the Americans watched the Japs misuse machinery, struggle with engines that had broken down, and tinker childishly at faulty motors; and they laughed at the Japs' inefficiency. However, it was no laughing matter for the people when, instead of using modern machinery, the Japs forced the Guamanians to pull rock crushers and build and level airfields by hand.

There was one note that puzzled us. Occasionally all the Guamanians would agree that some particular Jap was a good Jap; he had liked the Guamanian people and had tried to help them. Dr. Sablan, for instance, had a sympathetic word for the Kohatsu doctor, who he said had been kind to the Chamorros. Father Calvo told us about the Japanese Catholic priests. And men and women whom we liberated in various parts of the island seemed to want us to know that there had been some humane Japs on Guam who had tried to ease the people's lot.

For instance, near the village of Yigo we found a middle-aged woman who could scarcely wait to tell us how the Japs had mistreated her. Once, she said, she had gone into a Jap office in Agana and had seen one of her friends working for the Japs. She had stuck out her tongue at her friend, and a Jap officer had seen her. He ordered her to stand in the middle of the square in Agana for three days with her tongue out. It had been the most torturous ordeal, she said. Yet she hastened to add that her guards in the square had been most kind to her, that they had brought her water and sympathized with her and had pretended most of the time not to be watching her so that she had been able to rest her tongue.

On another occasion a Guamanian man told us how certain Jap civilian officials had smuggled rice into the concentration camp near Yigo for the people, after the Jap military guards had told the internees that they were going to be left to "starve to death for the flies."

"They brought the food to us at night at great personal risk," the Guamanian said. "If they had been caught, they would have had their heads cut off."

One day one of our patrols in the northern jungle came on a gruesome sight. A Pfc named Joe Young, a scout on the patrol, told us about it.

"We were trying to find out whether any Japs were bivouacked in the area," he said. "We went about two thousand yards forward, then about a thousand yards to our left, and were then going to turn and come back into our own lines. The jungle was very thick. It was quiet and ghostly. And it might have been my imagination, but there was a bad smell in the air.

"Suddenly we came to a clearing. There, spread out on the ground, were about forty bodies of young men. They had their legs drawn up against their chests and had their arms tied behind their backs. They lay in awkward positions—on their sides and their stomachs, and on their knees—like swollen, purple lumps. And none of them had heads, they had all been decapitated. The heads lay like bowling balls all over the place.

"There was a truck nearby with more bodies and lopped-off heads in it. It looked as if the Japs had been loading all the bodies and heads into the truck, but had been frightened away and had left everything behind.

"At first," Young went on, "we thought they were Jap soldiers, killed by their own men in some sort of harakiri business. But then, by the clothes, we knew they were young Chamorran men. There was one beheaded woman in the truck."

Before the bodies were buried, many of us visited the frightful scene and saw the victims of the Jap atrocity. A Guamanian youth told us they were men who had been taken from the concentration camps, charged with being American spies.

"That's the Japanese way of bringing civilization to people!" he said bitterly.

Later we told a Jap prisoner about the atrocity. He clucked his tongue and shook his head sadly.

"It was the work of Obuka," he said. "He is a bandit—a beast."

The Guamanian people agreed that Obuka, who had been head of the Jap secret police on the island, was their worst enemy. He was supposed to be still alive. Obuka, the people told us, was feared even by the Japanese.

By the time we reached the island's northern shore and announced that Guam was secured, we were on close terms with the Chamorros. We now had the job of returning them to their homes and farms and helping them to become self-sufficient once again. But with Obuka and many thousands of Japs, including all kinds of fanatics, running loose through the jungle, we could not consider Guam really secured. The people had no guarantee of safety. Also General Larsen had a schedule for building Guam into a large new American base, and he could not do this with so many hostile enemy about.

The people were anxious to help us clear the island of the remaining Japs. We needed their aid in what lay ahead of us, and we now welcomed it.

VI

In the Boondocks

SOON after Guam was called secured, General Larsen moved his Island Command headquarters to the ruins of Agana and set up the administration under which Guam was to be converted into "another Pearl Harbor." Tremendous changes were envisaged for the immediate future. The plans were ambitious; to us, living in foxholes in the thick jungles of the island, they seemed fantastic. But we were to play an important part in their realization. We were to guard the Seabees and engineers and rear elements who would pour onto the island and make the changes. We were to stay in the jungle, miles away, and continue fighting the Japs until the enemy was completely eliminated. A giant modern American base was to go up practically over night behind our backs, but we were not to see it rise. We would be too busy fighting in the boondocks.

The northern half of Guam was a wilderness—jungles, brush, coral caves, a few clearings of tall grass, and much mud. Marines called such country "boondocks." In most places the jungle was thick with pandanus, breadfruit, papaya, and other tropical trees and with heavy, matted underbrush that limited visibility to a few feet. Among the roots of trees a man could hide undetected for days. A few dirt roads ran through the jungle, linking what had been small native settlements. The Japs had used the settlements as storage centers, and our artillery had practically blasted all of them off the map. Along the coast were cliffs that dropped abruptly hundreds of feet to thick coconut groves and the sea. The cliffs were pocked with caves, hidden by underbrush, and the entire shoreline was framed by a treacherous reef.

Somewhere among these fifty-odd square miles of boondocks there were now thousands of Japs, disorganized and leaderless, hiding in caves and trying to stay alive. Most of them were confident that their fleet and air force would soon return and rescue them. Some were in large bands that eventually merged with others and accepted junior officers as leaders. Others were isolated individuals, cut off from their units and friends. Most of the enemy survivors were military personnel—soldiers, sailors, laborers, and special troops. A few were terrified civilians who had fled from Agana and followed their forces into the wilds. The more fanatical of the enemy were resolved to continue the fighting, attacking us in guerrilla fashion. Others seemed only to want to evade us, to be left alone. When we pursued them and discovered their hiding places, they fought back like trapped animals.

Many of the island people volunteered to help mop up the Jap remnants. The Guamanians knew the terrain thoroughly, some of them having had farms there. They knew the caves and the best hiding places. And they wanted to kill Japs. General Larsen armed them, and they came to our camps in the jungles to help us.

Two of our regiments, the 3d and the 21st, drew the assignment of staying in the boondocks and hunting the Japs. After the arduous campaign, the men were not overenthusiastic about the extra job, which meant continuing living in muddy foxholes and putting up with the discomforts of front-line combat duty. "They're making damn garrison troops out of us," a sergeant grumbled.

But it was more than garrison duty. It was still combat.

Again I was transferred and this time left the 9th Marines to go into the boondocks and join the 21st. The 21st was the outfit that had borne the brunt of the big Jap banzai charge on the ridge above the beachhead. During the campaign it had suffered about a thousand casualties. It was under the command of a square-jawed, soldierly-appearing Texan, Colonel Arthur H. Butler of El Paso.

The 21st had about half of the approximately fifty square miles to cover. The unit's headquarters and weapons companies were near Finegayan, where the 9th had run into its ambush. The three battalions were scattered, miles apart from each other, in the jungle. It was the rainy season and the boondocks were a miserable place in which to live. Each outfit had its own camp, consisting of a few fly and pyramidal tents for offices and mess-halls, and an area of foxholes covered by ponchos and shelter-halves. The ground was always muddy and the holes full of water. The camps were circled by barbed wire on which our men hung tin cans that clattered when the wire was moved. Our units maintained listening outposts, connected by telephones to the camps, and kept guards continuously alert around the bivouac areas.

All day long, and during the night, for weeks, the men went out on patrols, scouring the jungle and cliffs systematically, beating the brush and looking for enemy bands. When they weren't patrolling, they worked on the camp and stood guard in shifts. This was no rest period. We snatched sleep the way we snatched it in combat—in brief periods here and there. Most of the time we were wet and muddy; our bones ached; we were lonely, cut off from civilization. In one way it was worse than Bougainville: the folks back home thought the battle of Guam was over. And no one could tell them differently; censorship was on, and we could not send word home that the Japs hadn't given up. Mother and Dad might think that Willie was now getting a well-deserved rest and fresh food, which made Willie's job twice as difficult.

During the first weeks of mopping up there were fierce skirmishes in the jungle. Many of the Japs were still fighting back, trying to ambush our patrols. At night our men dug in wherever they were, established perimeter defenses (circles of foxholes) and waited for the Japs to attack in the darkness. Often they were not disappointed. Some of our units encountered wilder experiences than those they had met during the actual battle for the island.

One night during a torrential downpour a patrol was attacked by a drunken band of Japs. Our men were dug into foxholes around a temporary camp in the jungle. It was so dark and rainy that the Marines could hardly see, but they could hear the Japs moving up near the foxholes trying to find them. Finally the Japs made deliberate noises, hoping the Marines would fire and give away their positions.

One Jap screamed: "Hey, Joe! Hey, Joe!" above the roar of the storm. Another beat on a tea-kettle with a spoon. A third crouched by the Marines' water trailer and jabbered in Japanese. Our men eventually made out his form, but they were afraid to fire at him. They had to fill their canteens from the trailer in the morning, and it was all the water they had. They didn't want to puncture the vehicle and lose the precious water.

To add to the Marines' misery, the rain began to fill their foxholes. As the muddy water rose, they had to lift their heads, in order to avoid drowning; but by risking exposing themselves above the lips of their holes, they were in danger of being shot.

The Japanese at length grew tired of waiting. In the pouring rain they suddenly leaped to their feet and rushed at the Marine positions. They were armed with swords, sticks, and rifles; one man even had a hammer. This was what the Marines wanted. They mowed the enemy down. In the morning there were twelve dead Japs around the water-filled holes.

In another wild night fight, one of the most dramatic episodes of the entire Guam campaign occurred. A nineteen-year-old corpsman, Pharmacist Mate Third Class James H. Dierkop, was sharing a foxhole with two Marines, Sergeant Ruben C. Johnson and Pfc Gene Toffanetti. At about one in the morning, in a driving rainstorm, the Japs attacked Dierkop's unit. Somehow a Jap reached the edge of the corpsman's foxhole and jabbed his bayonet into Johnson. The sergeant screamed and kicked his feet at the Jap. Toffanetti, who had just awakened, grabbed the first thing he could reach —a shovel—and heaved it at the Jap. Then someone else fired. The Jap dropped a grenade and ran. The enemy.grenade exploded, and Dierkop, who was in the middle, was hit in the chest.

Despite his wound the corpsman turned to Johnson, who had been bayoneted through the kidney and spleen. While Toffanetti stood guard with his automatic rifle, Dierkop tried to help Johnson. He gave him morphine but had trouble stopping the blood. Finally, unable to stop it with compresses, he placed a poncho over the sergeant and stuck his fingers into the wound. All night long in the rain, he lay beside Johnson holding his fingers in the bayoneted man's side. Presently the blood stopped flowing. When dawn came, Dierkop, weary and almost numb, summoned a doctor. The wounded man was found to be bleeding internally and was not expected to live. Evacuated and sent to a hospital, he eventually recovered; the corpsman had saved him. Dierkop's own wounds were minor, and he was soon back with his outfit.

Many times the Japs boldly attacked our larger camps. One night a band of enemy hid in the brush near the RTB of the 21st Marines. The RTB—Regimental Train Bivouac—was a central supply depot for the entire regiment, set up somewhere between the rear dumps and the front lines. It was like a way station that collected and forwarded food, ammunition, water, and other supplies to the battalions. The RTB was manned by cooks, ordnance men, quartermaster, transportation, and ration personnel, and regimental supply officers. A group of our men wandering too near the brush that night were fired on. One was killed, and the others could not reach his body without exposing themselves to enemy fire. The dead man lay near the brush all night. In the morning his body was retrieved, but the Japs had fled.

Another time a band of Japs wriggled through our wire somehow after dark and charged into a galley. The startled cooks seized their weapons and stood in the open firing point-blank at the enemy. The Japs seemed to have gone crazy. They raced in circles with no apparent aim, screaming and yelling in Japanese. All of them were cut down within a few seconds.

As we continued killing Japs, our various units kept box scores showing how many enemy they accounted for each day. Our patrols toured through the jungles, searching isolated huts and setting ambushes wherever there were signs of recent Jap occupancy. Often they would surprise large bands of Japs and engage in pitched battles in the grass and among the trees. Sometimes they would catch a handful of enemy in a cave or around a hut and wipe them out before the Japs could fire back. The men got many souvenirs this way—both battle flags and sabers.

Some of our units had narrow escapes. Once a three-man reconnaissance patrol descended a steep, five-hundred-foot cliff to establish an observation post in a coconut grove near the beach. About one hundred yards away they saw twenty men in swimming. From where they were, the patrol members couldn't make out whether the swimmers were Marines or Japs. They decided to return to the brush and quietly walk parallel to the beach so as to circle nearer and find out who the swimmers were. They were just coming even with them when they ran smack into an outpost of seven Japs, resting by a rough lean-to of brush and guarding the swimmers. Before the Japs could jump up, the startled Marines fired a few rounds, then turned and raced away, thinking that the seven guards and all the swimmers would come after them. When they reached the cliff, they scrambled up it as fast as they could. Fortunately the Japs did not try to follow them and they escaped.

Another time a sergeant named Joseph J. Egnatovich got caught in the jungle between Jap and American fire during a fire-fight. He saw an abandoned Jap foxhole and jumped in. A moment later two Jap riflemen ran up, unaware of Egnatovich's presence. As they reached the foxhole, he shot them both. Several minutes later a third Jap ran up and Egnatovich killed him. By then the sergeant had had enough of the hole, and he left.

Our patrols were often helped by war dogs—German shepherds and Doberman pinschers. We had a platoon of them. Each dog had a skilled handler, a Marine who liked dogs and took care of the animal assigned to him as if he were looking after the welfare of a general. The dogs and their handlers, who were also something of scouts and snipers, were assigned to the different rifle companies during the battle. The dogs' specialty was sniffing out men who were ahead of us; they were good during advances or patrols in the jungle and in guarding our camps.

One day a twelve-man patrol was resting at the edge of a jungle clearing. Suddenly their Doberman pinscher, Rocky, began to growl. Alerted, the Marines discovered five Japs, armed with hand grenades, less than ten feet away. The enemy had crawled through the underbrush to take the Marines by surprise. The patrol members killed the Japs without themselves suffering any casualties.

In some instances the individual bravery of our men helped to increase the totals of dead enemy on the box scores kept by the different units. In Company I of the 21st Marines there was a daring little automatic rifleman, Corporal William A. Garron, who was known as "Trouble" because of his contempt for danger. On both Bougainville and Guam he had stalked many Japs through the jungle, walking cockily into situations that other men might have chosen to avoid.

One day in the boondocks Garron came swinging down a jungle road alone, a Garand rifle over his shoulder. He came on a patrol from another battalion. The patrol was hiding in the brush, drawn up in a circle around a tangle of trees that lay in the center of the jungle. The patrol members had tried to move in on the enemy, but every time they showed themselves they had been shot at by the concealed Jap.

Garron's nose tilted higher as he studied the brush. Then abruptly he unlimbered his Garand and pushed quickly into the jungle. The patrol members yelled after him, but the only reply was Garron's noise as he waded through the underbrush toward a big uprooted tree.

The Marines waited breathlessly. Then there was a shot.

At the base of the tree where the roots made a natural entrance-way, Garron had gotten the drop on a waiting Jap. But the little corporal had seen a sudden scampering of other enemy. He caught a glimpse of four brown-skinned men falling over each other, trying to find hiding places in the roots and branches. Firing point-blank he charged in at them, killing three before they could get out of his way. The remaining Jap dove out of sight behind the tree roots. Garron pushed after him cautiously. Suddenly he spotted the head of a Jap who was trying to see around the roots. The little Marine let go a final bullet. It killed the last enemy.

Returning to the path, he motioned back toward the tree. "Okay," he said to the patrol leader. "You can go ahead now."

The astonished leader was even more bewildered when he found the five dead enemy among the bushes. By that time Garron had gone on his way. The patrol leader didn't know who the corporal had been, but assumed that he was a member of his own battalion; so he added the five Japs to his battalion's box score for the day. Garron probably would have said nothing about it if the other battalion hadn't claimed the Japs. But now he claimed them for his battalion. Finding his buddies skeptical when he announced what he had done, he went over to the other battalion. There the patrol leader readily admitted Garron's claim, and the five Japs went on

GOING TO IWO JIMA. *Aboard our transport, off Iwo, we follow the progress of the units already ashore, wondering whether they will need us.*

THE BEACH AT IWO. An invader's-eye view—a barren, sandy, fire-swept slope, leading upward to the first airfield.

Company I's box score. Garron later received the Silver Star for the feat.

There were many light moments in the jungle also, humorous incidents that helped to keep the men more cheerful than they might otherwise have been. Once a big BARman went into a clump of bushes on a routine search for Japs. There were not supposed to be any Japs in the vicinity, and the BARman's companions lolled in the grass waiting for him. Suddenly they heard a burst of shots in the brush followed by a commotion. The BARman raced out of the bushes with a little bespectacled Jap chasing him, swiping at his heels with a long saber.

"Shoot the son of a b——!" the Marine screamed. "My BAR's jammed!"

The startled men rolled in the grass with laughter at the sight of the little Jap chasing the big Marine. One man threw his rifle, and another finally killed the little enemy with a carbine shot. The anguished BARman never lived down the episode.

Another time a flame-thrower made his way cautiously up to the mouth of a cave in which a Jap was known to be hiding. It was a dangerous spot to be in. The flame-thrower had to advance on the cave from behind the cover of some rocks, then jump into the open, and, before the Jap could fire at him, shoot his flames into the cave. It would be touch-and-go for the flame-thrower. He made his way slowly and carefully to the side of the cave, then leaped into the opening. He aimed his flame-thrower at the Jap and opened up. Instead of flames shooting out, a stream of liquid shot into the Jap's face; the oil had failed to ignite. With a frightened yelp the flame-thrower turned and tried to run to safety. When he fell over some rocks he thought it was his last moment on earth. The liquid, however, had blinded the Jap, who also turned and retreated deeper into his cave—and the flame-thrower escaped.

We also had adventures with animals in the jungle. On a patrol one day a private was in the center of one of our columns. The jungle was deathly still and our men crept slowly through it, scarcely brushing a leaf. Their senses told them that Japs were near by. Suddenly a terrific force struck the private in the seat of his pants and hurled him ten feet through the air to the base of a tree. Dazed but unhurt, he opened his eyes. A billy goat trotted unconcernedly past him.

Another time a group of men in Company E, the 21st Marines, received a brief respite from the work of patrolling. Many pigs roamed through the jungle near where they were camped, and they decided to try to get one for a barbecue. A gunnery sergeant sent out a three-man patrol for a porker. After a while there were shots in the woods. A little later the patrol returned—crestfallen: they had come on some Japs and had killed two, but they had found no pig.

Alarmed over the report of Japs near by, the gunnery sergeant sent out a twelve-man patrol. Hours later that patrol returned. The results were perfect. No Japs sighted, but one forty-pound wild pig caught and slain.

On another day, a corporal in the same outfit, who was known as "Chili Bean" because of his dark complexion, came on a thatched hut in the jungle with a sign outside reading: "Marines, please keep out." The corporal looked into the hut and saw two Japs calmly plucking the feathers from two newly killed chickens. Disregarding the sign, "Chili Bean" killed the Japs and brought the chickens back to his outfit.

Many of our patrols were helped by the native Guamanians. The 1st and 3d battalions of the 21st Marines were guided by a rugged youth named Felix whose family had suffered under the Japs. In his twenties, Felix looked like a prizefighter, with heavy eyebrows and tightly drawn lips. His father had been an American sailor who had retired, settled on Guam, and married a Chamorro woman. He had become wealthy and had owned a lot of land in the northern part of Guam. Felix had many brothers and sisters. Two of the sisters had married Americans; one sister had gone with her husband to live in the United States, while the other had stayed on Guam with her husband—a United States sailor. When the Japs came, they took Felix's father and the sailor to Japan as prisoners. Felix's mother died during the occupation. Another sister was mistreated by the Japs, contracted tuberculosis, and died soon after our liberation of Guam. Felix wanted revenge. He knew the northern part of the island, where we were hunting the Japs, like a book. He became a guide for us as well as a one-man punitive expedition.

Again and again he led us to caves and jungle retreats where Japs were hiding and participated in our fire-fights and ambushes. Every time he killed a Jap himself he notched his rifle after the tradition of the old Wild West scouts. Often he went after Japs himself. He found trails they were using and lay in wait for them. When they came by, he attacked them, choking many of them to death with his bare hands. Like many of the other Guamanian youths, he had little fear of the Japs, but rather contempt and hatred. Sometimes he took a Marine along with him on his personal adventures. He would go for the Jap; the Marine would go for the souvenirs. Felix's closest friend was a cook from Jersey City, a tall, wiry youth who soon learned so much about scouting from the Guamanian that he might have been Daniel Boone's son. The two men went off on forays into the jungle in the evenings and on Sundays, and rarely returned without having trapped and killed at least one Jap. The cook came back with flags, sabers, and other souvenirs. But Felix was interested only in his new notches, whose number soon reached the hundred mark.

One of our outfits was also helped by a Korean who had been a laborer on Guam for the Japs, and who had surrendered to us. We called him "Butch Roosevelt." Well educated and intelligent, he stated clearly for us the position of the Korean people: His people were enslaved in his homeland by the Japs and had to work and fight for them; but, though the Japs had occupied Korea for as many years as most of its people could remember, the Koreans still hated them and, if given the chance, would fight for independence. "Butch" wanted to become a Marine and go on with us to Japan and Korea. We kept him a long time in the jungle, where he helped us find Japs, but finally we had to send him back to Island Command for work with that organization. He went off in Marine clothes and equipment, loaded with gifts showered on him by the friends he had made in the outfit. He had also earned a lot of money working for the officers and doing jobs around the camp. We heard that the men up at Island Command were flabbergasted when he arrived. From the message they received, they had expected merely "one captured Korean"; what they got was practically a Marine.

As the weeks passed, we could see that we were making progress. We had been killing several hundred Japs a day; now we were only getting twenty or thirty a week—the survivors were fewer and fewer. Moreover, the stragglers were beginning to run out of food and supplies, and the ones we were killing were scrawny. Many were starving to death. Earlier they had been living on coconuts, breadfruit, papayas, bananas, chickens, and pigs; now everything except coconuts and breadfruit was getting scarce in the areas in which they were hiding. Sometimes they couldn't even find breadfruit, and a steady diet of coconuts is not substantial. More and more, the sick, weakened, and ragged Japs began to take risks, looking for food. Many raided our camps and dumps, trying to pilfer K and C rations. We waited for them and cut them down in the open.

Killing Japs near our camps created another problem. We had to bury the dead before the flies came. In battle there had been special burying details—a nasty assignment that most men tried not to draw. Now the regulation was posted that each dead Jap would be buried by the man who killed him. Many attempts were made to evade this regulation. Nobody stopped trying to kill Japs, but many tried to sneak away from the

dead enemy before anyone could establish who had fired the
fatal shot. Often there were arguments between Marines,
usually boastful about their marksmanship, but now anxious
to convince each other that they had missed the dead Jap by
a mile.

One unit found a solution to the problem by appointing a
single man as the official burier. To make the job attractive to
him, the commanding officer ordered that, if there were any
souvenirs to be had from the dead enemy, the official burier
would have first choice, no matter who had killed the Jap.
The burier used to sit in the camp waiting for shots. As soon
as he heard one, he would be off like a flash into the woods to
be sure that the man who killed the Jap didn't steal a souvenir
before *he* could take first choice. The other men used to tease
the burier by "test firing" in the jungle. When the burier
would dash up out of breath with his shovel, they would grin
at him and holler: "Test fire!"

As the jungle became safer the Chamorros began to drift
back to their homes and farms. Island Command let them
keep firearms with which to protect themselves, and many
found use for them. Once, near one of our camps, a sixteen-
year-old boy named John Benevenda came on three sickly
Japs in an abandoned hut near his farm. He fired five shots
with his carbine, riddling one of the Japs through the chest.
The other two enemy ran away.

As August and September passed, our loneliness and misery
in the boondocks continued. We heard of the campaign on
Peleliu and looked forward to the invasion of the Philippines.
We knew that the pressure of offensives elsewhere was preventing us from receiving fresh food and other supplies that
men might expect following the conclusion of a hard campaign. The ability of the Japs to hang on in the jungle
irritated us; the longer they remained, the longer we would
have to remain where we were. It was no mystery to us how
they hung on. They were sick and starving and sometimes

thirsty, but, like men who have made up their minds to fight a disease, they had steeled themselves to the prospect of living in the wild terrain as long as possible. And meanwhile our letters from home kept referring to the "rest" we were having.

One day one of our patrols came on an abandoned Jap food dump hidden in the jungle. Crates of dried fish and sacks of rice were piled up among the trees. Near by, a well-worn footpath showed that Japs were coming there regularly. We hid among the bushes during the day, but no enemy appeared. That evening we formed a twenty-man patrol and set an ambush around the dump. The patrol was under the command of a young, light-haired First Lieutenant, James C. Corman.

It was late in the evening when we dug into foxholes in a circle covering the path, two Marines in each hole. Many were armed with BARs; the rest had Garands, carbines, and pistols. We were told not to shoot until the enemy was directly on us. If an enemy broke through the circle into our center, no man was to shoot inward; we were to rely on knives.

Darkness descended on us while we were still digging. We were in a small clearing where bombs had knocked down the trees early in the campaign. The food dump was at one side among the jungle growth. The ground was bumpy and covered with debris—tree trunks, branches, coconuts, bushes, and old logs. As our men disappeared into their holes and became silent, it seemed as if the area was deserted. It was very ghostly and mysterious, since no two men could see any of the others.

I was in the remains of an old shellhole with a tall, nervous corporal named Walter Page, one of my closest friends, who had been through Bougainville. He had once studied to be a priest but had changed his mind and had joined the Marine Corps. He was the most argumentative person in our outfit, but he was also one of the kindliest and friendliest. He would do anything for anyone and expected nothing in return—an unusual quality that made him something of an oddity in the Marine Corps. Also in the hole with us was Lieutenant Corman. There was not quite room for all three of us, because we hadn't had time before dark to dig the shellhole larger. So we lay on the slopes, half exposed above ground. We hoped our bodies would blend with the logs and debris lying around us in the open.

Each of us stood or rather, lay guard for an hour. Page and I had pistols, and the Lieutenant had a carbine. But it didn't matter whose turn it was for guard; none of us slept. The mosquitoes attacked us in droves and, despite our headnets and mosquito lotion, covered us with itching bites. We didn't dare scratch, for fear of making a noise, but lay hour after hour in agony.

It was a nightmarish scene. The jungle assumed a thousand shapes, each seeming to move stealthily as we stared through the gloom. There were noises of all kinds—twigs snapping, leaves rustling, grunts and squeals and sudden coughs—and every one made us jump as if an enemy were about to appear. We eventually realized that the noises came from falling coconuts, banana rats scampering across the ground, and wild pigs rooting through the underbrush. Once a cow pushed through the trees. We held our breaths. It sounded like a patrol of Japs. We could see a shape in the darkness, edging among the trees. It came nearer, and we saw what it was. We swore at it under our breaths.

A little before midnight I began to doze. On my back, with my head resting inside my helmet, I was on the slope, half in and half out of the hole. Page was on top of the hole on his stomach, his chin was resting on the dirt; he was gazing straight ahead. Suddenly he began sliding back towards me. He moved his arm back slowly, pinched me, and without turning his head whispered calmly: "Here they come. Look out."

I didn't dare turn on my stomach. Arching my head back, I looked upside down at the path. The full moonlight on the little clearing gleamed through the trees and lit up the path. Four figures were moving down it, coming toward us and talking in low voices. Two carried rifles. They were completely unaware of our presence.

I looked across our shellhole. The Lieutenant was pressed against the dirt on the opposite slope, breathlesly watching the approaching Japs. Slowly he pushed his pistol out ahead of him. Then his hand twisted it into firing position. We waited tensely as the Japs came nearer. Finally they were less than ten yards away, about to turn into the ration dump.

A BAR, almost beside us, shattered the night with a frightening roar. Red flames from the muzzle blinded us. The next instant there was deathly silence, and the blackness returned. A few yards away we could hear a moaning.

Page looked back wildly.

"One down," he whispered. "Where are the other three?"

We lay as quietly as we could, listening to the wounded Jap moan. We looked around at the black shadows, wondering what had happened to the other three enemy. Obviously we weren't in a good position. The other Japs, two of whom might have been the ones with the rifles, were probably hiding in the trees, waiting for us to make a motion and reveal our position. The moonlight was streaming down on us in the clearing; while we couldn't see the enemy, it would be easy for them to see us.

We quivered in terror. The wounded Jap's voice began to rise in a singsong prayer. It was like a baby's voice crying— high and sad. We could hear the mosquitoes buzzing in our ears and feel them stinging through our dungarees; but we couldn't scratch. A coconut crashed in the jungle, and our hearts beat wildly. Still no sign of the other Japs. The smell of dried fish filled the clearing.

Suddenly we heard a tapping—like metal on a rock.

"Duck!" Page breathed.

The next instant there was an explosion and a blinding

THE SCENE ON SHORE WHEN WE LANDED. Men, supplies and equipment filled the small beachhead. Jap mortar and artillery shells couldn't miss.

LOOKING NORTHWARD FROM SURIBACHI. Landing ships are pouring supplies ashore for use. Swarms of men and equipment are headed north, toward the Iwto-

flash. Pieces of metal and flesh and chunks of dirt rained down on us. The singsong prayer was over—the Jap had blown himself up with a hand grenade.

We stayed quiet and on guard the rest of the long night. The mosquitoes tortured us. After a while the dead Jap, lying a few feet from us, began to smell. The odor joined with that of the fish in a stench we could never forget. We peered around at the trees, trying to find the other Japs, but they had vanished.

When dawn came, we poked warily about. No one fired at us, and we concluded that the three Japs had run off when our BARman had first fired, leaving their wounded companion behind to commit suicide.

The dead Jap lay among scattered salmon cans and a toppled crate of dried fish. He had no head—he had held the grenade against his face, and all that remained was his scalp, which had fallen down across his throat. His body was full of holes from the BAR. Flies swarmed around the bloody clothes and the open flesh of his wounds. Big toads sat on his neck and his limbs, darting their tongues at the flies.

In the Jap's wallet we discovered a torn clipping from an overseas edition of *Time* magazine which the Jap had probably picked up after a Marine had thrown it away. The clipping was a picture of Japanese-American soldiers fighting with United States forces in Italy. We would have given a lot to have known what the dead Jap had thought of the picture.

Before we left the scene, we buried him and burned the food dump. When we reached camp we reported one dead Jap for the night: not a good score. We didn't know how our BARman had missed hitting the other three enemy. He didn't know, either; he said he was nervous and tired.

And he could be taken at his word. There's nothing like the jungle to make one nervous and tired. The jungle is terror. Stalk and be stalked. That night we had set an ambush and had ended up as though we were the ones being ambushed. And that was only one patrol; the same kind of thing was happening day after day, night after night.

And back home the Battle of Guam had been over for two months. . . .

VII

Some Japs Surrender

BY THE end of September we were getting tired of our patroling, and our commanding officers were as anxious as the men to end the monotonous mopping up. Then, one evening, we took an important prisoner.

One of our patrols came in with Captain Yamaka Moriji of the Imperial Japanese Navy. A man of fifty-nine he was then, I believe, the highest-ranking prisoner we had taken in the Pacific war. But he looked like any other Jap straggler on Guam. His clothes were soiled and tattered after weeks of roaming through the jungle. His face was dirty and unshaven, and he was weak and thin from hunger. Our men had come on him unexpectedly. The little old fellow was in the open, plodding down the center of a jungle road. When he saw the Marines, he drew himself up stiffly and raised his arms to show that he wished to surrender.

By the insignia on the Jap's stained uniform, the Marines could tell that they had an important prisoner. He asked them in perfect English, with a trace of Oxford accent, to take him to our General. The Marines were proud and excited. Enemy officers usually just disappeared or were found dead; here was a real live one—something to boast about. The men hurried him back to battalion headquarters where his rank was ascertained. Put on a truck and driven to our regimental CP, he was ushered into Colonel Butler's tent, where he introduced himself as a meteorologist who had been supervising the construction of a weather-reporting station on Guam. He was disturbed over his appearance and asked for permission to wash and shave before continuing the interview; it was undignified, he said, for a Japanese officer to appear before our commander in an unkempt condition.

Colonel Butler, a firm but just officer, let him wash and offered him a plate of C rations and a cup of coffee. The prisoner ate slowly and gratefully—it was his first real meal in days. He said he had been living "like an animal" in the Guam jungles ever since Japanese organized resistance had collapsed a month before. He had been on Guam only a short time when the Americans had landed; before that he had been in Soerabaja, the big Java naval base.

Colonel Butler listened to him soberly; there was something on our regimental commander's mind. The Jap was an intelligent man—scientist rather than militarist. In his education and travels he had come in contact with Western thinking and customs, and he seemed more logical, by our standards, than any of the other Japs we had captured.

"Why did you surrender?" Colonel Butler asked him.

"I had a very good Javanese friend," the Jap replied, "with whom I discussed for hundreds of hours whether death in war was preferable to surrender. He believed that the Japanese custom of regarding surrender as unthinkable was foolish. I disagreed with him vigorously. But when I found myself living like a wild animal and slowly starving to death, I realized that I had been influenced by his arguments."

"Do you think that other Japanese would surrender if they knew that we treated them honorably?" Colonel Butler asked.

The Japanese officer nodded in a businesslike fashion. "In my opinion," he said, "we have fought an honorable fight to the end, and we have been defeated. The battle is over now. If it were known that the Americans treat their prisoners according to justice, perhaps more Japanese would surrender."

Later this officer was sent to Division headquarters and then to Island Command. There he was interviewed by Generals Turnage and Larsen and shown personally the same fair and honorable treatment we were according the prisoners we already had in our stockade.

His capture gave impetus to our efforts to get more of the Japs to surrender voluntarily. We thought we could speed the process of straggler elimination by inducing other Japs to do as the Captain had done. It amounted to a new relationship between ourselves and our enemy—an incongruous relationship that bewildered a lot of our men.

Since the early days of Guadalcanal, we had learned not to trust Japs who wanted to surrender. There had been too many cases of treachery. We had heard some terrible stories. One concerned Japs who surrendered in pairs. Just as they reached the Americans, one man would fall on his hands and knees, revealing a light machine gun strapped to his back. His companion would man it quickly, shooting down the startled Americans. Another story was of Japs who surrendered with their arms upraised, only to hurl grenades from under their arm-pits into the faces of their would-be captors.

Such Jap duplicity was the fault of the enemy's leaders. We knew that they had a policy of preventing their men from surrendering by telling them that the American "foreign devils" tortured and killed their prisoners. The fear thus generated, combined with the traditional notion that surrender is dishonorable, made most Japs prefer suicide to capture. The suicide, of course, was always the more honorable if it could cause a few American deaths. In battle, therefore, we learned to live by the rule of kill or be killed. We refused to risk our own safety by exposing ourselves in tests of the good intentions of Japs who indicated a wish to surrender. In face-to-face encounters we knew that the man who shot first won—and lived.

This is not to say that we never took prisoners. When the issue was clear-cut—when, as in the case of the Japanese

Captain, it was obvious that we had the situation in hand and were not risking our lives by allowing a man to surrender—we brought the man in. During our initial landing on Guam, for instance, we found a Jap sitting on the beach, dazed by our D-day bombardment. It was a simple and safe matter to take him back to one of our ships as a prisoner. We had also captured many wounded Japs during the fighting on the island—men who were too injured to put up resistance. And, finally, at the time we took the Jap Captain, we were beginning to bring in sick and starving men who could hardly stand up without our help. Our patrols were finding them lying in cave entrances or in the jungle. Sometimes they were asleep, as in the case of Takahashi Yoshiki, a young Domei News Service war correspondent whom we found in a coma in a native hut. He had fled from his office in Agana and had tried to live on with the remnants of the Japanese troops in the jungle. If we hadn't found him and given him food and medical care, he would have starved to death.

But to most of the Marines, accustomed to a fanatical enemy who preferred death to surrender, our new policy was at first puzzling. We dropped leaflets from airplanes into the jungle areas and tacked them to trees alongside paths. They told the Jap survivors in their own language that they could keep their lives and honor by surrendering.

"Do not be afraid," our notices read. "You will not be harmed. Advance alone and unarmed to where American troops are located with your hands up, stripped above the waist, carrying this leaflet and walking down the center of the road. Those who do so will receive food, water, and medical treatment."

The Japs must have been puzzled, too, for the results were not encouraging—few availed themselves of our offer. Those who did were mostly frightened civilians who had fled from their businesses and homes in Agana and had taken refuge in the jungle with their troops. They were not so thoroughly disciplined as the others, and our leaflets made more sense to them than staying in the woods and starving to death. They sneaked away from the small bands of fanatical soldiers with whom they were traveling and, following our orders, gave themselves up. But the bulk of survivors—Army and Navy men—continued to hold out.

One day on a patrol we saw two Jap soldiers approaching down the center of a narrow road. When they spied us they paused. Suddenly one of them fell in a heap on the road, while the other ran into the brush and disappeared. Suspecting a trick, we advanced cautiously. Three members of the patrol took up positions to guard against our being ambushed, and the rest helped lift the Jap to his feet.

He was a sack of bones and rags, half-starved to death. He cringed against a tree, hesitantly nibbling at a chocolate D-bar offered him by one of our riflemen. We heard a jeep approaching down the road. The noise startled the Jap, and he collapsed again in terror. When we took him back in the jeep, he recovered enough to tell us that the Japs still thought we would torture and kill any man we caught. Their propaganda had been too strong; they did not believe our pamphlets.

We decided the Japs needed proof of our promises. Our idea was to use sound trucks—regular transport trucks, rigged with a loud-speaker system. Jap prisoners who had received good treatment from us volunteered to go along. As the truck toured slowly through the maze of jungle roads, the prisoners talked into a microphone in Japanese, telling any Jap who could hear the blaring loud-speaker that the Americans lived up to their promises. The prisoners presented themselves as evidence of our good faith and talked of the food, water, and medical treatment we had given them.

This plan produced a better effect. The Japs, hearing the voices of men they knew, began appearing in greater numbers on the jungle roads, stripped to the waist and waving copies of our leaflets. Our old veterans were astonished. They referred sarcastically to the truck as a "vote-getting truck" and complained that it broke up their ambushes. One of our patrols heard the sound truck coming through the jungle one day. The patrol was hiding in the brush near a hut that showed signs of recent Jap occupancy. The infuriated patrol leader sent a runner to the road to tell the truck to get away.

"Damn it!" he called. "They'll scare all the Nips out of here."

The truck kept going and an hour later returned up the same road. The patrol was still waiting for some Japs to appear—the truck had four prisoners!

The voluntary surrenders made sense. Anything that speeded up the tiresome mopping-up period and got us out of the boondocks, back to rest camp, seemed reasonable. The men shrugged and decided to give the Japs a chance. The fellows in the line companies, still on the alert for Jap deceit, watched the prisoners for false moves. There were none. Our prisoners increased.

Some of the Japs surrendering told us that most of the survivors were hiding in the dense coconut groves and rugged terrain below the cliffs lining the northern shore. This posed a new problem for us: We had to get into where the great numbers of them were; but it was a particularly wild and inaccessible area, cut off from the rest of the island by sheer 600-foot coral cliffs. There were no roads into the area, so we couldn't drive our sound truck in. The only way to reach them was from the water.

That was where the "Peace Ship" came in—one of the strangest vessels in the Pacific war. The "Peace Ship" was an LCI (G), a small green landing craft that had launched rockets at the Japs all through the Guam battle. She was under the command of a young Baltimore officer and had a young, tough crew who lived and fought informally, as is the custom on the small amphibious craft of the Navy. There were two old salts aboard: Chief Boatswain Mate John D. Henderson and Boatswain Mate First Class Ernest L. Adamson. Between them they had seen action in almost every naval engagement

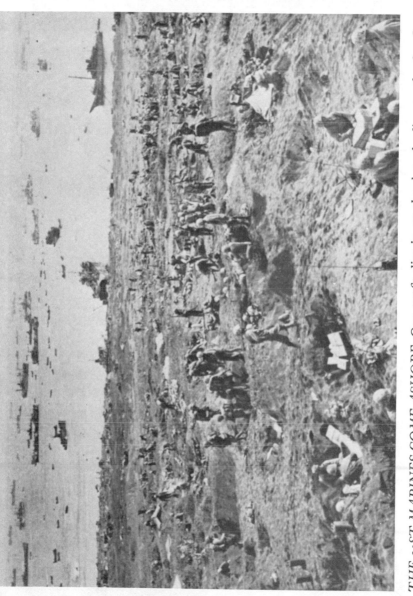

THE 21ST MARINES COME ASHORE. Our outfit digs in on the slope leading to the first Iwo airfield. The next morning these men went into the lines.

UP THE TWIN LINES. Our men leave the beach headed for the lines before the second airfield, Suribachi.

and amphibious landing since Pearl Harbor. Henderson had
been with the Asiatic Fleet when the war broke out and had
fought in the early disastrous battles around Singapore and
Java. Adamson, in the Central and South Pacific, had been in
all the Solomon Islands fights; he rated sixteen battle stars.

After so much action against the Japs, the two regular
Navy men felt peculiar when they were told that their little
gunboat was to be used to lure enemy survivors on the
northern coast into surrendering. They watched us when we
came aboard and rigged our public-address system in one of
the gun tubs, pointed all the guns of the ship skyward instead
of shoreward, and hung colored signal flags and pennants to
all the lines.

"Damned if it ain't a peace ship," Henderson said.

The name stuck.

The LCI's job was to cruise back and forth along the reef
opposite the coconut groves where we suspected the Japs
were hiding. A Jap prisoner, who had volunteered for the job,
would call to his fellow-countrymen through the public-
address system with the same sort of appeal we had made from
the trucks. As an added measure two other prisoners would be
rowed across the reef in a dinghy from time to time and left
ashore by themselves to enter the coconut groves, find some
Japs, and try to prove to them that the Americans were acting
in good faith. We could hardly have been more liberal in
showing the enemy our good intentions, for we were actually
releasing—on their honor alone—two prisoners of war who
might very well choose not to return to us.

Henderson's and Adamson's astonishment soared when the
first Jap came aboard and was quartered in the same hold in
which they slept. He was a little brown-skinned fellow with
big, pouting lips—a comical-looking monkey—and at first the
seamen stared curiously at him and laughed. Then he, too,
began to grin and chatter in English. He knew a lot of our
words, particularly our slang, which he had learned from
the Guamanian people. He explained that he had been a

chauffeur for a high Jap naval officer on Guam, but, more important, he had met and fallen in love with a native Chamorran girl. That had gotten him into trouble with his commanding officer, who felt that he should have nothing to do with the people of the island. When he persisted in seeing his girl, he was thrown in the Jap brig for two months. When he got out, he said, he felt friendlier than ever towards the Guamanians. He learned English with their help and, when the Japs put the people in concentration camps before we landed, he had been one of those who had smuggled rice and dried fish in to them. During the fighting his car was wrecked by a plane; so he abandoned it and hid in the jungle alone until he could get word to his girl that he wanted to surrender to the Americans. She finally arranged it and led one of our patrols to his hiding place.

Like the rest of the crew, the Chief and Adamson were intrigued by the little Jap's friendliness and good nature. He told the sailors his favorite people in the world were Babe Ruth and Judy Garland, and he amazed them by quoting American big-league baseball batting averages from past years. He said he had no family left in Japan and that after the war he hoped to come to the United States where, as he put it, no big guy would push him around.

"What do you want to do?" Ernie asked him.

"I want maybe to be mascot on the New York Yankees," the Jap replied.

From then on he was the most popular person aboard ship. The sailors gave him the free run of the vessel. They showered him with candy, clean clothes, and cigarettes. And they gave him a name—Joe. The word spread around the harbor that there was a "savvy" Jap on board the LCI, and other seamen flocked to see Joe. His reputation spread from ship to ship, and he was soon a legend throughout the harbor.

The other two Japs were more quiet and reserved. They were the ones who had volunteered to be rowed ashore, while Joe would do the hollering through the loud-speaker. One of them, whom we will call Nito, had been a schoolteacher in Saipan and then a civilian paymaster for the Jap Navy on Guam. His job had been to pay for civilian supplies and labor. When the Americans shelled Agana, he fled with a considerable sum of money. A Navy plane strafed his car. He dropped the money and ran into the jungle where he remained until he surrendered. He was about thirty-five and spoke German and English. He was slightly effeminate in his gestures and manner of speaking and acted as if he had not wanted any part of the war. He was still somewhat shocked at the experiences he had gone through on Guam, particularly our shelling and the days he had wandered around starving in the northern jungles. Although he had surrendered voluntarily, he had been frightened not only of us but of the other Japs—particularly the fanatical Navy officers: he was afraid they would kill him if they ever caught him. Oddly enough, that is why he had volunteered to go back in the jungle. He would show himself to them as a gesture that he had not lost all his honor. If they killed him, he would be receiving his just punishment. If, instead, they chose to do what he had done and surrender, it would again be what fate wanted to happen and he would be spared.

The third man was named Taki. He was a slight youth with long hair and delicate features. He had been a soldier, used to taking orders. He had little to say and did his best to stay out of everyone's way. When we passed him, he bowed low. When we looked at him, he smiled apprehensively and glanced quickly away as though he expected an ax to fall suddenly on his neck. He had come from a poor peasant family and had had little schooling. Nito was teaching him English.

I accompanied Taki and Nito from our stockade to the harbor. We drove in a closed Marine carryall. Both men gazed out of the windows all the way, astonished at the American activity and equipment that were converting Guam into a great base. In a month we had done more on the island than the Japs had done in their two and a half years of occupation. The prisoners, who had gone straight to the stockade from the northern jungle where they had been captured, had not seen all the heavy American equipment working in our rear. The streams of trucks and bulldozers that we now passed impressed them, and they shook their heads and clucked their tongues bewilderedly.

Passing through the ruins of Agana, we paused momentarily for traffic. A group of Guamanian people saw the two Japs beside us and flocked angrily around our car. A toothless old woman picked up a stick and waved it at our window. We shooed them away and started off again.

Nito turned with a polished, polite smile on his face.

"Thank you," he said. He sucked in his breath when he talked. "They hate the Japanese, don't they?"

We nodded, and he shook his head helplessly. "I hate the military too," he said.

We went aboard the LCI and set out that evening for the northern coast. We had orders to stay out three days. We took with us three members of our joint assault signal company, young fellows who had been with the front-line rifle companies, directing naval gunfire on targets found by the infantry. They had had many rugged experiences during the campaign and had seen a lot of their buddies killed. They were now to stay in communication with Marine patrols on top of the cliffs. If we spotted Japs who would not surrender, we planned to guide the patrols down the cliffs to where the Japs were hiding. We would tell the Japs that they could choose between surrendering to us and sure death from the Marine patrols. The Jasco boys—as we called the members of the joint assault signal company—were skeptical. They still hadn't been sold the idea of wasting time on trying to get Japs to surrender. However, they were glad to get out of the mud and jungle for three days and welcomed the sea trip and the fresh Navy food.

Early the first morning we sighted smoke from a campfire,

rising above the coconut trees. Joe manned the public-address system and called on the Japs to come out of the grove and surrender. He had a high, strong voice that carried over the water.

"Nipponese!" he shouted. "Come to the beach and give yourselves up to the Americans. The battle is over. The Americans are treating those who surrender with honor. Do not starve to death. The Americans will give you food and water and medical care. I have surrendered and can promise you all these things."

A solitary Jap poked out of the bushes and stared at us; then he disappeared. We decided to put Taki and Nito ashore to try to talk to the Japs personally. Ernie and Henderson rowed them across the reef in the little dinghy and landed them on the sand. The sailors told the two Japs that the LCI would sail out of gun range to show that we meant no harm. Then, in a couple of hours, we would come back to pick them up. Nito said that he would try to have many Japs waiting for us on the beach when we returned. He was frightened, but he tried to control his emotions.

"If we are not here," he said stoically, "you will know we have been killed." He smiled feebly and, followed by Taki, plunged into the jungle.

When we returned two hours later, we found three Japs waiting on the sand with Nito and Taki. Joe was excited. He leaped to the public-address system.

"Congratulations, brave and honorable Nipponese," he called. "You will not regret your decision. The Americans will treat you well according to their promise. You will get good food—A-number-1 American rations. Fine doctors will care for your wounds if you have any. Your days of suffering are at an end."

Henderson and Adamson got into the dinghy again and started towards the reef. But the surf had become rough. A squall was approaching. The sky was gray and cloudy, and the wind was already howling. The water, which had lapped peacefully across the reef earlier in the morning, was pounding furiously over the sharp, hidden rocks. The small boat bobbed around like a cork. Henderson tried twice to take it over the reef but saw that it was too dangerous; it would be hurled on the rocks and smashed.

"Tell them to wade out," Ernie called to us.

Joe shouted directions through the loud-speaker to the Japs on the beach. They understood and slowly entered the water. We noticed that two of the Japs were wounded; they carried wooden staffs with which they supported themselves.

It was about one hundred yards from the beach to the reef—a long, treacherous wade. The water boiled furiously as the waves rolled in from the rocks. In some places it was a foot deep, in others almost up to the Japs' shoulders. The wounded men were nervous. Twice we saw them turn back, but Nito and Taki urged them on. The wounded men acted as if they suspected they were being deceived. It therefore became a matter of honor to Nito and Taki to prove that the Americans would not let them die. They helped the wounded men through the bubbling surf, struggling arm in arm, slipping on the coral formations, and almost falling as the waves hit them. The two sailors watched anxiously from outside the reef.

Suddenly one of the wounded Japs toppled over and, losing his staff, floundered helplessly in the water. The current swept him in circles against the sharp rocks. Henderson stood up in the dinghy and shouted at the other Japs to save him, but they were having troubles of their own. Henderson told Ernie to hold the little boat steady, then he lowered himself over the side and went to the rescue. While Ernie held the dinghy as close to the reef as possible without cracking it, the Chief swam through the angry surf, crossed the coral, and reached the struggling Jap. By now the other wounded man was also down. Henderson threw his life jacket to the first man and grabbed the second one by the arm. Half-carrying and half-towing the two, he guided them through the water and across the reef to safety. Ernie helped pull them into his dinghy and rowed them to the LCI; then he returned for the others.

It was a strangely happy scene of reunion when everyone was finally aboard the LCI. Nito and Taki were proud of their achievement in finding three of their fellow-countrymen and talking them into surrendering; and happy too, that they had proved to the other three that the Americans would keep their word and return and save them. All five showed an ironic sense of comradeship with the Chief and Ernie, as if they felt they had been on the same side in a common struggle in the water and had triumphed.

When Ernie and Henderson went below to their hold to change into dry clothes, one of the Jasco men went with them. "Congratulations," he said. "Nice job!"

Ernie and the Chief looked at each other and laughed.

"You sure are getting to be a Jap-lover," Ernie said kiddingly to Henderson.

"You would have done it yourself if you hadn't been on the oars," the Chief answered.

And Ernie probably would have—despite the sixteen times he had met the Japs in action.

The squall blew over us and went on its way, and we picked up more Japs in the afternoon. Ernie and the Chief kept rowing them back to our fantail. They would be hoisted aboard, scared that we were going to kill them. We would make them undress—which increased their terror. But when we handed them soap and hosed them off with salt water, they knew they weren't going to die immediately. We gave them clean Navy skivvy drawers and shirts, and our pharmacist's mate looked them over and dressed their wounds and jungle sores.

They were all in bad physical condition. For weeks some of them had been living on coconuts and breadfruit alone. Their bones showed through their skin, and their stomachs were distended. Many had open wounds which they had been unable to clean or properly dress. A young soldier had a mortar-fragment wound in his shoulder that was full of maggots. Another Jap—a Navy laborer—had a bullet still in his leg; he had been shot by one of our patrols a week before.

The prisoners were also filthy dirty from their days of living in the bushes. Their matted hair was full of lice, and their legs and feet were covered with running sores. We sprinkled them with everything from sulfa powder to the new DDT, which had just come out to the Pacific. Before throwing the Japs' clothing overboard, we searched it and told the prisoners they could keep their personal articles. However, they gladly gave us the battle flags that they had worn around their waists beneath their undershirts or in their puttees, as well as some Japanese coins they had—which meant much to our sailors, who rarely had a chance to procure souvenirs ashore during a battle. The only thing they wanted to keep was their little prayer books.

We gave them a full meal of rice, chile con carne, corn, coffee, and canned fruit, which they gobbled up, smacking their lips appreciatively. Then we put them on the forward deck, where they squatted down out of the way and studied their tiny prayer books, still believing that sooner or later we would kill them.

In the middle of the afternoon I accompanied the Chief and Ernie on one of the trips ashore. It turned out to be one of my strangest experiences overseas.

We had seen a single Jap emerge from the jungle. He stood motionless on the beach a few moments, listening to Joe's harangue. Then he sat down abruptly and crossed his legs. We took it to mean that he wished to surrender.

We started ashore to get him, Nito going with us in the small boat in case we needed an interpreter. As we skimmed across the reef we studied the Jap on the beach. He carried no weapon but had several hand grenades, and a bayonet was hooked to his belt. When we were about fifty yards from shore, the Jap stood up and began kicking coyly at the sand.

He turned around and looked at the brush and then at us, as though he had something on his mind.

Nito, uneasy, told us to stop rowing. He gazed at the man on the beach, then told us to head for another part of the sand, about a hundred yards away, and let him get off alone.

"He is fanatic soldier," he said to us, sucking in his breath importantly. "Very dangerous. He has grenades. Maybe kill me for surrendering. Maybe kill you too."

Suddenly it struck us that, among the three Americans in the boat, only I had a weapon—a sheath knife. In an effort to show the Japs that we were sincere and meant no harm to those who wished to surrender, the Chief and Ernie had been coming in unarmed.

We needed no prodding to follow Nito's directions. Turning, we headed up the beach a hundred yards from the Jap and put Nito ashore.

"You wait here," he said.

As he walked down the beach to his compatriot, we sat in the boat, prepared to shove off and row back to the reef at the sign of any hostile move. We glanced longingly at the LCI, wishing it could offer us more protection. Festooned with its gaily colored flags, and with all its guns pointing skyward, it looked more like an excursion craft than a warship.

Nito reached the Jap soldier and offered him an American cigarette. Then they sat down and began to talk. Every so often we could see them look at us. Finally Nito got up and came back to us.

"He wants you to get out of the boat and sit on the sand. Show you have no guns," he said.

We looked at each other. At such a moment the full danger latent in a situation is not always apparent, and you make snap decisions that later make you wonder whether you were in your right mind at the time. Without hesitation we got out of the boat, pulled it up on the sand, and sat down. Nito nodded and walked back to the waiting soldier.

We watched them over our shoulders, but tried not to let

them see that we were nervous. We pretended to be looking for shells in the coral sand, but all the time we were planning mentally how to get into the boat quickly and shove off before the Jap could rush us with a grenade. Once or twice I looked down the beach and saw the two Japs arguing violently. I kept imagining that the soldier was fingering the grenades, getting ready to spring up suddenly and charge us.

Finally the soldier jumped to his feet. We turned and held our breaths. He looked at us an instant, threw down his cigarette, then turned abruptly and disappeared into the brush. Nito got up slowly and made his way back to us. There was a sad look on his face. He held out his hands and sighed.

"He had no wish to surrender," he said. "We go back to the boat."

We were so relieved to be quitting the beach that the strangeness of what had happened didn't fully dawn on us. It was only as we were crossing the reef that we learned how lucky we had been.

"Well, we gave him a chance," Henderson said. "Now I hope the patrols get him."

Nito shook his head. "Oh, he surrender some other time perhaps. Right now he cannot. Many other fanatic Japanese in bushes, watching. If he try to surrender, they shoot him. Japanese soldiers all around beach there." A thought suddenly struck him, and he smiled politely. "Good they no shoot you, hey?"

By the end of the first day we had talked sixteen Japs into surrendering. They were quite a burden for our little LCI; we would gladly have returned to our base and handed them over to the MPs. But we had orders to stay out three days. Also we wanted to get an early start again the next morning, which would have been impossible if we made the round trip back to the harbor.

So we looked all over the cramped ship for a convenient place to quarter the prisoners during the night. Finally Ernie suggested putting them down in the hold where we slept. Henderson and I didn't like the idea very well. The prisoners were still crawling with dirt and sores, and they smelled like bad fish. One gnarled old fellow—a Navy worker—had a terrible case of dysentery from the coconuts on which he had been existing, and it had brought on bleeding hemorrhoids. Ernie compromised with us and quartered the old man in another compartment where the pharmacist mate could look at him every so often. The others were herded down the ladder to our clean, whitewashed hold and shown where to lie down against the bulkheads on either side.

Our Jap interpreters—Joe, Nito, and Taki—didn't enjoy the presence of the prisoners any more than we did. Joe, who had thrived on the way we had accepted him into our friendship, was jealous of his position and wanted no competition from other Japs who might endanger his status. Nito and Taki, on the other hand, were uneasy over being quartered with the men they had urged into surrendering. They were still nervous lest some of them develop a change of heart in the middle of the night and try suddenly to murder them.

We therefore put the prisoners on the opposite side of the hold from Joe, Nito, and Taki, and placed a member of the LCI's crew between them as a guard. Ernie gave the prisoners lifebelts (for pillows) and blankets, and, using Joe as interpreter, ordered the prisoners to stretch out beside each other. Nito and Taki sat on their bunks across the way, watching the men nervously.

When I took off my pistol belt, Nito urged me to keep it next to my pillow. "It is safer," he said.

Joe heard him and laughed at the schoolteacher's anxiousness. We were inclined to agree with Joe. The prisoners looked harmless. Most of them were still nervous and scared, still expecting us to kill them. They watched us guardedly, noting our every movement and scarcely daring to breathe.

Gradually, as Henderson, Ernie, and I began to talk nonchalantly among ourselves and as the guard stopped watching the prisoners and took up a magazine, they became less tense. A few of them lifted themselves on their elbows and ate some soda crackers that we had given them at chow. They crunched the crackers noisily between their gums and smacked their lips to show their enjoyment. The noise irritated us and Ernie told them to cut it out. When they showed they did not understand him, Joe jumped up and, as if to show his authority, hollered at them in a stream of irate Japanese, until they cowered against the bulkhead and stopped their gum-smacking. A little later they began whispering among themselves. Out of the corners of our eyes we noticed that they were sitting up, admiring a metal ammunition can that Ernie had brought down to use as a wastebasket. As the jabbering increased, Henderson turned to Nito.

"What's bothering them?" he asked.

"The metal," Nito said with his polite smile. "In Japan metal is scarce. It surprises them to see it used as a basket."

"We've got lots and lots of metal—millions more tons than Japan thinks we have. You tell them that," Henderson said.

Nito digested the thought, then told the prisoners. They listened eagerly, and when he had finished there was a murmur of interested "Ahs!" This encouraged Henderson to pass on some more facts through Nito, and he started a description of our great war production—the thousands of tanks and guns and planes and ships that the Americans were turning out, the big war factories spread over thousands of miles in the United States, and the stream of equipment that would arrive to be thrown against Japan as soon as the war in Europe was over. Nito nodded and passed each item on to the prisoners. They sat up slowly and murmured and shook their heads as if it were all too much to believe. They turned to each other and began to argue, and then asked Nito for more information. Henderson passed it on eagerly—about our big convoys, getting larger each month, about all the new kinds of American landing ships, about the hundreds of thousands of U. S. Marines who took the places left by the men lost by

America earlier in the war, and about our great army that was tearing across France.

As Henderson talked, Ernie got out a pony edition of a recent *Time* that fortunately had some convincing pictures. He showed Nito a shot of G.I.s raising an American flag in Paris. Nito exclaimed in surprise and passed it eagerly among the other Japs. It somehow made him feel better, as if it helped to justify his own surrender and the way he had urged the others to give up.

Even Joe was interested in the facts we were enthusiastically volunteering. He was already a hundred-percent believer in whatever an American told him, but each new fact continued to entrance him.

"See?" he said to little Taki, as if he were giving our information himself.

Taki nodded happily, as if his life too had taken a turn for the better.

Suddenly one of the prisoners startled us by speaking out in English. He was a tall, thin man with a wispy black mustache that curled down over his lips.

"I wish to thank you for telling me all this," he said in a sharp voice. "I have no doubt that you are speaking the truth, for I too know America. I was a cook on a ship that went to the United States, and I have been in Galveston, San Francisco, New York, and Washington, D. C. I have an uncle who owns a restaurant in New York City. I would like to go there after the war."

He glowered at the other prisoners as though he expected them to lunge at him. Then he berated them suddenly in Japanese. After a moment, during which we tried not to look startled, he turned back to us and announced that he had known all along that the Japanese leaders were lying to the people.

"They are bandits," he snapped. "They lie to us all the time. The American fleet is sunk, they say; the American army is destroyed; Japanese soldiers are in Washington. And all the time they are waging war through us for the profit of the Mitsuis and Mitsubishis. *They* are the only ones who gain —the people suffer."

Joe suddenly bounded up and gestured at the cook as if he were going to hit him.

"Sit down, Joe," Henderson laughed.

Joe sat down snarling, jealous of one who not only seemed to know more than he did but also was using his knowledge to wriggle over to the Americans' side.

The cook was an intelligent addition to our dramatic bull session. The incongruity of what was occurring—a frank, uninhibited discussion between captors and prisoners, between men who had been used to fearing and hating each other—was lost in the closeness of the little hold. Ernie, delighted by the Japs' willingness to talk, passed around a pack of cigarettes, and some of the prisoners nodded their heads politely and accepted smokes.

"No doubt," Ernie said, "the Japanese lied to you about the treacherous way your Navy attacked us at Pearl Harbor?"

The cook looked puzzled. He puffed silently on his cigarette, staring at Ernie. "I do not understand," he said.

"Don't you know that Japan attacked the United States without warning at Pearl Harbor and Wake Island and the Philippines?"

"While your so-called ambassadors, Nomura and Kurusu, were talking peace in Washington?" Henderson added.

The cook hissed thoughtfully and nodded. "Ah," he muttered. "We were told the United States fleet was coming to attack us in Japan. We struck back and halted the Americans." He turned to the other Japs and spoke quickly to them. Then he looked back at Ernie. "Please tell me. Am I wrong?" he asked.

"I should say you *are* wrong," Henderson said. "Tell him, Ernie."

While the Japs waited for a translation, Ernie told the cook of the anger aroused in the United States by Japan's sneak attacks.

"The whole United States was united against Japan," Ernie said.

The cook nodded and translated to the other prisoners what Ernie had said. They whispered excitedly, as though a great truth had broken on them.

"So," the cook said. "I have cooked for the deceitful Japanese Navy. I would like to cook for the United States now."

Ernie laughed. "I'm afraid that's impossible," he said. "But after the war you can go back to Japan and tell all the people there the truth."

The cook's face fell, and he became silent.

"We can never return to Japan," Nito said. "None of us. Ever."

"Why?" Henderson asked.

"Because we have surrendered."

The cook nodded.

"That's silly," Henderson said. "Before the war is over, we'll invade Japan, and every Japanese will have to surrender. Then there will be no difference between you and them."

Nito and Taki shook their heads violently. "They will not surrender," Nito said.

"Now that's just another lie they've told you," Ernie insisted. "Do you know that all the people up on Saipan surrendered to the Americans?"

Nito stared at him, but showed that he did not believe it.

"We are dead men," he said. "We can never return to Japan."

Joe saw our puzzled looks. It gave him a chance to get in a word. "It is this way in Japan. When a Japanese surrenders, it is considered that he has committed dishonor. Then it is considered that he never lived. One must forget him completely. His wife and his poor mother and his children erase him from their memories. No memorial is placed for him. It is not that he is dead—it is that he never existed. Naturally, he can never return to Japan."

"Silly," Ernie said.

"More," Taki nodded with an awed look on his face. "After death—no paradise."

"You go to hell?" Ernie asked.

"Hell?" Joe repeated. "No hell." He shook his head. "There is no hell for the Japanese. But no paradise either for him who surrenders. Nowhere to see again one's wife and mother and friends. There is nothing. Everything is finished. It is terrible!" He paused, looking seriously at us. Suddenly he smiled. "I do not believe any of that. I don't care what they do in Japan. I don't want to go back."

Nito and Taki abruptly launched a stream of Japanese at him. Joe hissed back at them, then looked at us again and grinned. "They still believe it," he laughed.

The cook cleared his throat authoritatively and hunched forward. "It is true," he said. "One cannot return to Japan."

"But look, fellow," Henderson said, trying to make the thing clear to them. "If everybody back in Japan surrenders, then there is disgrace for everyone—no?"

None of the Japanese answered. It seemed too hard for them to comprehend.

Henderson tried again. "Now you agree, your leaders lied to you about the war—right?"

The cook nodded slowly.

"All right. Maybe they lie about your not being able to go back to Japan."

The cook stared at him. Suddenly Nito said, "Ah, yes. Maybe."

"Now, just for instance," Henderson continued, "why are you fighting in China? Why do the Japanese attack the Chinese people?"

The cook was angry again. "For the Mitsuis and Mitsu-bishis," he barked. He turned to the other Japanese and

PAST THE FIRST AIRFIELD. We move along the edge of the first Iwo airfield, scarcely noticing the piles of wrecked Jap planes.

PINNED DOWN. Caught between the first and second airfields, our men huddle in the soft volcanic ashes.

lectured to them quickly again in their language. They nodded understandingly.

Joe listened to them, then voluntarily translated it to us. "He says the war against China is unjust and full of lies."

"That's right," Henderson said. "The Japanese want China. But China belongs to the Chinese—the people who live there. Savvy? You understand?"

Joe nodded. So did Taki and Nito.

"I have never agreed with the war in China," Nito said with an obsequious grin. "America for America, Japan for Japan, and China for China."

"That's right," Ernie said.

"And don't you see," Henderson continued, "if the Japanese leaders lied to you about China, they can also lie about your not going back to Japan?"

In the silence that followed, as the prisoners tried to understand what Henderson was telling them, I could see for the first time the mental torture through which these men were passing. In a moment of weakness and spiritual confusion, they had surrendered, had committed a dishonorable, cowardly act which they could never undo. They had crossed a Rubicon, so to speak, and could never go back. Now, if they kept on believing their leaders' propaganda, they were forever doomed.

I thought back to the many isolated, cornered Japs we had seen fighting like wild animals from the Guam caves. The issue they had faced became suddenly clear. To die honorably and go to paradise, or to surrender and face eternal damnation? I looked suddenly at Nito, the esthetic, almost effeminate schoolteacher. A few days before, he had been something dangerous and hunted—a Jap enemy stumbling wildly through the Guam jungle. To us Marines he had been one with all the weird, half-human visions of men who live in caves on fish and rice and shoot Nambus at passing Americans, and then blow themselves up with their one remaining grenade.

"Have you any children?" I asked Nito.

He drew out his wallet and handed me a small, yellowing studio picture, pasted on a card: the portrait of a young-looking Japanese woman in a flowered kimono, with two small children in robes and with bangs over their foreheads. The man in the picture was Nito, stout and wearing a civilian suit.

I handed the picture back to him. He was smiling modestly. For a moment it was impossible not to think of my own family, my wife and year-old daughter, back in Washington.

Suddenly I had an urge to ask Nito the one question that had been shaping in my mind during our discussion.

"Tell me, Nito," I said. "If you had it to do all over again, would you have committed suicide instead of surrendering?"

He looked around embarrassedly. The other Japs didn't seem to understand my question. Nito dropped his eyes.

"If you give me a knife, I will kill myself now," he said.

"Good Lord, fellow!" Henderson exclaimed.

Nito looked up and saw that we were shocked. He thought he had offended us.

"I will kill you too," he added. "Then we can all go to paradise together as friends."

We Americans laughed, but we felt uneasy. I glanced around to be sure that my pistol belt was still on my pillow.

"He thinks that he would be doing us a favor," Ernie exclaimed.

Henderson leaned forward puzzledly. "Why do you fellows believe in this harakiri business?" he asked. "Maybe that's more lies, huh?"

Joe drew back startled, and I laughed. It looked as if we had suddenly stumbled on ground sacred even to Joe.

"It is bushido," he whispered in a tone of reverence.

"Bushido," Henderson said. "You explain that, huh?" he pointed at Nito.

Nito shook his head sadly. "Please," he said. "I could argue with you all night trying to convince you that Christianity is all superstition and untrue, and that there was no such person as Jesus Christ. I might even force you to say you believed me. But in your heart you would not be swayed. You have been born to it and raised and educated to it. In the same way you could argue with me all night trying to prove that bushido is wrong, that harakiri is senseless. But you cannot convince me. It is my faith and my spirit. I am Japanese. I was born and brought up Japanese. I cannot change." He looked away.

After a moment Henderson got up.

"I guess we'd better get lights out," he said. He turned to the guard. "They won't make trouble. But don't let any of them make a move."

After I had undressed and climbed into my bunk, I lay in the darkness listening to the heavy breathing of the men around me. One by one the prisoners fell asleep. I began to wonder if these people *could* change so that some day we could live in a world at peace with them. They had a lot of strange ideas—big ideas that had been drilled into them all their lives. It seemed to me, though, that there were bigger ideas in the world—ideas like freedom and democracy and justice and truth. With patience we could change the Japanese, and more quickly than most people thought. Even our little bull session had begun to work a change among the handful in our hold.

This was the present, however, and these were still Japanese enemies. Our tiny peek into their minds could be no more than a teasing prelude to what would come after the war. Before falling asleep I put my pistol beneath my pillow. It was bulky, but it made me feel better.

VIII

"We Didn't Come Here For Fun"

IN THE few months since we had landed on Guam, great changes had taken place on the island. At first the only times we had been aware of the changes were when we had left the boondocks to go back to the rear areas. Sections of the island behind us were unrecognizable. Large tracts of brush and jungle had been knocked down and cleared away. Wide, modern highways had taken the places of the narrow, twisting jungle roads. Native settlements had given way to Army, Navy, and Seabee camps and giant depots and dumps. The little road along our beachhead where our halftrack had been blown up on D-day was now a big four-lane highway. Where the Jap banzai charge had occurred, quarters were being built for the Commander-in-Chief of the Pacific, Admiral Nimitz. Office buildings were going up throughout the area, rising in the draws and valleys and on the hills where "Slug" Marvin and his flame-throwers had burned and sealed Japs in caves.

Every time we went back to the rear we rubbed our eyes with astonishment. The island seemed to be getting new units every day. And life was comfortable back there among the new arrivals. There were tents and huts and even wooden barracks in which to live. There were large mess-halls, libraries, theaters, and athletic fields. There was a beach for

136

swimming, where the reef had been deepened and cleared of mines. There were wine messes for officers; and dances with newly arrived Navy nurses; and showers and hot and cold running water. A terminal building was going up at the airport with a coffee bar and a powder room for women passengers. And lots of women were arriving on Guam in those rear areas—newspaperwomen, a Congresswoman, nurses, Red Cross workers.

Out in the boondocks we were still living in holes, still washing with rain water caught in helmets from the flies of our tents, still eating a hundred-percent canned food diet. But as the weeks passed, we saw civilization creeping closer to us. We noticed new camps springing up in the jungle around us —army engineer units, signal corps companies, quartermaster and service outfits. We saw new roads coming at us through the jungle, then whole sections of the boondocks disappearing. We saw long lines of bulldozers and carryalls, chopping at the jungle all day long and, by the illumination of hundreds of floodlights, all night long. Slowly we saw the boondocks being opened to the sun, great clearings made that ran three or four miles in length and a mile or two in width. And on the equipment of the men making the clearings was the identification: "Army Aviation Engineers."

It was exciting. No one had to tell us what was going on. The B-29s were coming to Guam.

As the jungle continued to disappear, civilization finally reached us too. Our rear echelon had by now arrived, bringing up our tents and seabags and bedding rolls. We greeted the men we had left so long ago on Guadalcanal, and answered their questions about the battle and about how some of our friends had died. We held no grudge against the men of the rear echelon, but we knew that, as far as Guam went, we were different, and there was little use trying to find common ground in a discussion of what we had done or what had happened to us.

The most important thing about the arrival of the rear

echelon was that we had some comfort again. We put up our old pyramidal tents in a grove of papaya and coconut trees and moved out of our muddy foxholes. It was a strange sensation, lying down on something soft again. All through the camp, we could hear men sighing contentedly, as they climbed beneath their mosquito nets and stretched out on their cots. Many of the men, however, were too used to the hard ground, and spent the first night rolling restlessly on their mattresses.

Although the jungle was fast disappearing, the more determined Japs continued to find places in which to hide. But often they had to leave their retreats and come out to look for food and supplies. Newly arrived troops on the island were startled by the Japs, and many of the enemy were killed by members of American units who had never thought they would fire a shot during the war; on their first night on Guam, for instance, some members of a startled laundry outfit shot two Jap stragglers.

Scarcely a night passed without our having an encounter with a stray Jap or group of Japs. One night one of our men claimed that he saw a Jap using a shower we had built. It was a tall wooden structure with a gasoline drum filled with water that sprinkled through a ration can punched full of holes. The Jap was probably stealing water to drink. When our man went after him, he vanished in the shadows. Another time someone spotted a Jap sneaking among a row of tents. Half the camp took up the wild pursuit, but the Jap vanished into thin air. The next day it was suggested that he had escaped by hiding in a Lister bag until we had given up the chase!

As we reduced our patrolling and guarding, we began to hold classes and once again took up combat training. The classes dealt with routine subjects like camouflage, demolitions, flame-throwing, and chemical warfare. We built coconut-log pillboxes on the fringes of the woods near our camp and practiced hurling smoke bombs in front of them and attacking the boxes with flame-throwers. One day we were startled to see a Jap standing in the woods watching us. He was so enthralled by what we were doing that we almost caught him. At the last moment, he came to with a start and slipped away through the jungle.

Between August 11—when Guam had been called secured —and the end of October, we killed more than five thousand Japs. But with all our mopping-up activities—our daily patrolling, our ambushes, and our efforts to get the Japs to surrender—we knew that there were more thousands still free on Guam. Most of them by now were in a desperate condition, and time would kill them. But there were still a few disciplined fanatics, able to take care of themselves and make trouble. If nothing else, they were still tying us up, since as long as they remained at large they were a menace to the many projects being undertaken by those building up Guam. Moreover, those projects were now getting under way in the heart of what had been the boondocks—in the very sections of the island where the Japs were trying to hang on. It would not do to leave them at large in that area as a constant danger and nuisance.

The whole 3d Division was now called out to fight what we referred to as the second battle of Guam. It was a "sweep," an operation that later became familiar to all troops who took large land areas from the Japs: a thorough and systematic attempt at mopping-up. Just before we launched it, our Division received a new commanding general. General Turnage returned to Marine Corps Headquarters in Washington for an important assignment, and Major General Graves B. Erskine took command. We had also been getting replacements to fill the holes left by our casualties during the Guam fighting. Many of the replacements were veteran Marines who had served with the 1st Marine Division at Guadalcanal or the 2nd Marine Division at Tarawa, had had a furlough in the United States, and had been sent overseas again. The rest of the newcomers were "boots," overseas for their first time.

The "sweep" was also designed to help work the replacements into the combat teams and give us all practice for something tougher that was supposed to lie ahead. What that was we didn't know. But there were many rumors, and they sounded ominous—something about "another Tarawa."

The sweep was launched by all three of our rifle regiments, stretched across the width of the island abreast. We started about even with Agana and worked northward, like a row of elephant beaters, combing the jungle. We moved in a line— each man within calling distance of the men on both sides of him, and each man moving in a straight line ahead, no matter what he had to climb, descend or cross. At night perimeter defenses were used, and guards shot at Japs trying to infiltrate the line.

We moved slowly, searching tangles of brush, and pausing to seal as many caves as we could. On paper it seemed inconceivable that any Japs could have eluded us. But as we progressed we realized that, hard though we might work, the job we had set out to do was impossible. There were stretches in the thick, matted jungle along the bases of the cliffs where the country was as formidable as any our men had ever seen. We groped and stumbled, trying to stay on straight lines, but were diverted by rocky walls, sharp coral formations, and steep inclines, all covered with masses of vines and underbrush. Footing was insecure, and travel was wearying. After a few hundred yards we were out of breath. Brambles tore at our faces and clothes. We cut our shoes on the coral and turned our ankles. The hot, tiring work weakened our resistance; we came down with malaria and dengue fever. Some of the men tried to go up and down the 600-foot cliffs, looking for caves in the sheer rocky wall; a few trips were enough for even the hardiest.

In this kind of terrain our combing was not so thorough as we had planned it. Gaps were left in our wall where rocks and jungle barred the men's progress. And through those gaps some Japs were able to make their way, particularly at night.

COMBAT FATIGUE. Out in the open, our men are subjected to uninterrupted pounding by the Japs. Nerves crack, and men, with casualty tags pinned to them, are ordered back for rest.

ACROSS THE SECOND AIRFIELD. Third Division Marines file across the newly-won second Iwo airfield. In the left foreground, we still duck ing Jap fire.

Also, our plans for sealing caves were too optimistically drawn. There were literally hundreds of them at different levels in the faces of the cliffs and behind the thick under-brush at the cliffs' bases. We blew some and explored as many of the others as we could. In some we found sick and wounded Japs; others showed signs of recent Jap occupancy but were empty when we searched them. We had teams of demolitions men with us who for ten days followed our lines, blowing one cave after the other. But to blow all of them would have taken several months and would not have been worth the time and effort. Nevertheless in some of the deep recesses of the more inaccessible caves we knew that we were leaving Japs who eventually would either starve to death or, coming out for food, would run into one of our camps and be shot down.

In some hiding places we found Japanese women who had fled into the jungle with small Jap bands and had shared their hideous hunted existence ever since. The girls wore anything they had been able to find—Jap army coats and pants, Marine dungarees, silk kerchiefs around their hair, split-toed rubber shoes, civilian knickerbockers, and brown leggings. Some were sick from the monotonous diet on which they had been living. Others were in surprisingly good health, with fat, rosy cheeks and big grins for our men.

Discovering Jap women was an exciting adventure, for many of the enemy girls were geisha girls. Geisha girls were something strange to us, something out of the pages of Oriental adventure stories, by-product of a civilization alien to ours; and our conception of them had been formed on a combination of rumor, fancy, and imagination. At first we thought that all Jap women on Guam were geisha girls. Most of them, instead, were respectable wives and members of families of Jap civilians who were caught on Guam by our landing. The fighting had alarmed them, and they expected that we would surely kill them. Some of them carried babies, and our men did everything they could to treat the enemy

women and children with kindness. But the geisha girls—
"comfort girls" is probably a more accurate name—didn't
appear particularly frightened when we captured them; as far
as they were concerned, one man in uniform was much like
another, whatever country he belonged to. Once a Jap woman
made advances to one of our scouts, Platoon Sergeant John L.
Riley, while he was taking her back to Division headquarters
in a truck. He was guarding her in the well of the vehicle,
and she tried to caress him.

"I told her she was a prisoner, but it didn't seem to mean
anything to her," Riley later told us.

At the end of ten days, we closed our final trap along the
northern shore and caught a handful of Japs in our pincers.
Altogether during the sweep we killed or captured several
hundred enemy. While some had continued to elude us, we
were sure that no sizable band of troublemakers remained.
The mopping-up period on Guam had ended. Among the
Japs who had escaped us, however, there were some who were
to make trouble later. Every so often, as the weeks went by,
small groups continued to reappear. In February 1945—six
months after the island was called secure—five unarmed
American sailors and a Chamorro, looking for bananas in the
jungle, were ambushed and massacred by a band of Jap
stragglers. And several months after that—almost a year after
we landed on Guam—a Jap officer emerged from the brush
and surrendered a small but well-disciplined group of Jap
soldiers, all in good health and with well-kept equipment.

One morning, after the sweep was ended and we had
returned to our camp, we awoke to find that we were
suddenly in the middle of a clearing. During the night bulldozers had knocked down the trees and brush in our area.
We were on what was to become one of the runways for a
B-29 field. We moved our tents a few hundred yards off,
only to have the process repeated several days later. Finally

we set up our camp on ground not marked by the army aviation engineers, and watched the airfield develop. We saw the ground leveled and asphalt laid; we saw hangars go up and mountains of crated supplies arrive. At length new camps were erected near us, and in came units of air corps men direct from the States—technicians, engineers, communications men, pilots.

Finally the big day arrived. The first Superfortresses of the XXI Bomber Command left Saipan to bomb Tokyo. On their return, we were told, many of the B-29s would land on Guam. During the afternoon we stood in the jungle at the edge of the airfield and waited for the planes we had never seen but about which we had heard wonderful things. Their coming meant much to us: they were the evidence of what we had accomplished in retaking the island, a part of the reason why our men had died. Moreover, we felt an attachment to the ground on which the planes would land. For we had taken that part of the jungle. We had fought through it and lost some of our buddies there. Beneath the asphalt also lay the bodies of Japs we had killed.

About seven o'clock in the evening the lights of the first big Superfortress appeared, and our hearts felt light and happy as we watched the long, graceful, silver plane circle over us and settle for the landing. Then other lights appeared —several dozen of them, belonging to the advance guard of the great team that was to pound the cities of Japan into rubble. They had been over Tokyo that very day—Tokyo, which had always seemed so very far away from us. For the first time we suddenly thought of it as being very near. We who had come from Guadalcanal were practically on Japan's front doorstep. We had made the jump in six months.

The first plane's wheels hit the ground at about the spot where we had once come out of the jungle from Tiyan airfield. It made us remember the days gone by. *There*, we told ourselves, had been, the road to Finegayan—no longer visible beneath the black asphalt runway. *There*, where the taxiing plane was roaring, was where our popular Captain Shoemaker had been killed by the Jap 77. And *here,* up near the hangars where the plane was heading, was where the Japs had had their two road blocks—where we had lost a hundred men, where Witek had died and won the Congressional Medal of Honor. *That* was where the radioman had said goodbye to me when he had relieved the other member of the forward observer team. And *there,* where the mechanics were running out, was the site of the little green house where our aid station had been, where all those men had lain on stretchers. *There* was where the jeep had pulled up with the trailer loaded with fresh shoes and dungarees. Remember the driver? "Them's for my boys," he had said. . . .

We saw the first B-29 stop, we saw the welcoming committee rush out in jeeps and weapons carriers to greet the flyers. And slowly we turned back into the jungle to our camp in the mud.

"There'll be steaks for those flyers tonight," one of our boys said.

That night we killed a Jap by the edge of the airfield. He too had had his first glimpse of a B-29. But he didn't live to tell anyone what he thought about it.

Now that there was no more daily patrolling, we had time to think. And it was not good for us. Most of our men had been overseas two years. With the exception of a few months, all of that time had been spent in the jungle, and the men were lonesome. They talked more of home, but in strange, unrealistic terms, as if people back home had had good reasons to forget them.

"I won't know how to talk to people back there," one man said. "It's so long since I've seen them."

Some of our men had stopped hearing from their girls, and that didn't help.

"They've got other guys," a sergeant said. "They forget what you look like. They think you're never coming back.

They drop you slowly. The first year they write every week. The second year, every month. After that, not at all."

Such brooding was to have its effect: to make us feel as if we were living in a vacuum, unattached to social units in the outside world. Few of us ever discussed what we were fighting for, how we had gotten into the war, or just what positive results we might achieve from it. Each man's life was a little world in itself, and personal happiness was the common goal. That happiness depended on the satisfying of needs—good food, comfort, love, family unity, peace of mind, and security. Whether it was actually true or not, to most men home was where those needs were satisfied. Home was where the family was, where the girl friend lived, where the food was good, where the bed was soft and the toilet was private. That was what we were fighting for.

The bigger questions, the political, economic, and social issues that would ultimately affect the realization of our dreams—these were "politics," and a little beyond us. We once had a man in our tent who had been a member of Colonel Evans Carlson's Raiders. Colonel Carlson had believed that a man was a better fighting man if he knew what the war was all about and why he was fighting. The Raiders had eventually been broken up and the men scattered through the various Marine divisions. The man in our tent used to talk of some of the things about which Colonel Carlson had lectured his Raiders.

"You fellows," he said to us, "are the guys who have to find jobs. You have to pay more dough if prices go up. You have to pay taxes. And if there's a war, you have to do the fighting. But you have no interest in politics. You don't care what the politicians do. You just take everything bad that comes along without finding out what made it happen or whether it could have been avoided."

True, but most of the men didn't seem to care. Perhaps their attitude was due to the combination of youth, lack of political education before going into the service, and the natural preoccupation of most Americans with anything but politics. Whatever the reason, their main concern was with home and their basic personal needs and desires. So it was important that home should remain the symbol of all that would satisfy our needs. We wanted it to represent the place where our girl was waiting for us, where the food was going to be good again, where there was hot water for bathing, where we would find jobs that would give us security.

When we weren't thinking about home, our minds were on the problems of the moment—the problems of daily life. In time of combat they were fixed on staying alive and carrying out military assignments. When we weren't fighting, little things grew into great problems: clean clothes, water in which to wash, a pencil with which to write a letter home. And, of course, the environment around us became the greatest problem of all.

I was in a tent with three other staff noncoms. We had no lights. Night after night we lay on our sacks in the darkness, trying to fall asleep, but kept awake by the warm and merry noise coming from the officers' wine mess on the hill where our officers had music, weekly liquor rations, and the companionship of nurses to help dispel their loneliness.

On every island in the Pacific, most enlisted men considered the presence of white women a problem. Only a few white women—nurses, Red Cross workers and an occasional woman war correspondent—came to the islands. Men who had been cut off from civilization for two years and had had their normal ways of life thwarted felt frustrated by the sight of the women. If only there were enough to go around! But there weren't. A few officers got the dates and the chance to mix with the women; the rest of the men stood around watching. Back home, every man could find a girl of his own choosing; in the Pacific it was different. A newspaper correspondent echoed the sentiments of the men in our outfit when he wrote that the perfect solution would be to send over enough women for everyone, or else none at all.

One day we heard rumors of another impending move.
Nothing definite was said, but we had been on Guam for a
long time; Guam was now a rear area; we were not garrison
troops, and there was no reason for our staying there longer.
We had more classes, and our training was more determined.
Our mortars and machine guns chattered on the ranges day
and night, and our rifle companies slogged along the road
singing, as they had once sung on Guadalcanal:

"Right now we are rehearsing for another big affair,
We'll take another island, and the Japs will all be there.
And when they see us steaming in, they'll take off on the run.
They'll say, 'Old pal from Guadalcanal, you didn't come here
     for fun.' "

Other people in higher echelons were making decisions.
We didn't know what was happening—whether we were
going, or, if so, where. Our men began to think of rotation.
Two years in the tropics was a long time. When would they
go home? Three of the men wrote a parody of the song
Embraceable You, called "Replace me, I can't go home without you," and dedicated it to Marine replacements still in the
United States. In the evening we compared scraps of information that each of us had gathered during the day, and
tried to put two and two together. Jerry Gruggen, a jeep
ambulance driver, told us that he had been ordered to have
his vehicle waterproofed and ready for loading by a certain
date. Our hospital corpsmen were seen packing medical
supplies—morphine syringes, combat dressings, plasma con-
tainers, and the new serum albumen cans. Our two regimental
chaplains went to a special meeting for all Division chaplains.
The Red Cross man assigned to our regiment began packing
—combat kits of toilet articles, cigarettes, corncob pipes. And
the rifle companies spent more time in the boondocks. We
saw them marching into the woods early in the morning:
Company I, led by tall, rugged-looking Captain Clayton S.
Rockmore, former Cornell football player; Company F,

under the command of Captain Gerald G. Kirby, a short, wiry Floridian; G Company, moved along by Captain Howard L. Cousins, who had helped break up the Jap banzai charge above our Guam beachhead; L Company, led by Captain Edward V. Stephenson, also a hero of the Guam fighting. These and the other companies of our regiment were filled with our friends, men with whom we had been sharing adventures and hardships. They were our buddies, the men who spoke our language, who had been joined to us, as closely as men could be joined, by perilous adventures.

There was "Trouble" Garron who had killed the five Japs in the boondocks; Martinez, who had lived through the banzai charge; Walter Page, who had lain beside me when we had tried to ambush the Japs in the jungle; and Joe Young, the scout who had found the bodies of the beheaded Chamorros. How many of these men and others were shortly to become casualties, to leave us forever!

Joe Young was typical of many of them. A tall, gangly Marine with a kindly disposition, his greatest love was his rifle, an outmoded Springfield '03. Joe paid more attention to it than he did to anything else. He kept it clean and shiny, always the best-looking rifle at our inspections. Joe had had to get special permission to keep his Springfield. The rest of us carried the newer and faster-firing Garand. But Joe liked the old bolt-action weapon; he claimed it was more accurate. During the Guam fighting he picked off Japs with it at three hundred yards—slowly, one after the other. Joe had neither family nor friends at home. His parents, he told us, were dead. Before the war he had done commercial art work in Baltimore and had planned to marry a certain girl. After he joined the Marine Corps, his girl made other plans, and he never heard from her. Joe was the only man in our outfit who never got a letter; there was no one to write to him. But he still wanted to go home. He had been saving his pay, and he wanted to begin over again in civilian life. After two years in the jungle, that life back home was important. It was opportunity to do something, to be somebody. It was the reason for living, for having been born.

Up and down the long rows of brown pyramidal tents, our men all had the same feelings. There was Platoon Sergeant Richard Naylor, who had joined the Marine Corps before the war. He had served in Iceland prior to Pearl Harbor. Now he had had enough of combat. He too wanted to carve a decent life for himself. And the same with Sergeant Robert P. Fowler, a squad leader who had done enough fighting on Bougainville and Guam for ten men; and with Technical Sergeant Ralph S. Nolley, a tall thirty-year-old Marine who had left a business career and a girl to come over and fight the Japs. There was another life back home for him too, a life with meaning.

Now, as we approached new combat, we began to wonder how long our men would be kept overseas. We went on long conditioning hikes, and we slowly realized that, until the war was finished, there would be no other life for us. This was our role, whether we liked it or not. We had come into the service for various reasons, and we had to keep going until somebody told us we could stop. Meanwhile, if life as we wanted to live it was passing us by, if we were getting older and not deriving what we wanted from it, that was our sacrifice, that was what we were giving up for somebody else. We weren't sure about it, but we hoped that some day it would all have meaning and would prove to have been worth while.

Among the replacements who had come to us was one man who made us realize how little we were actually doing. He was Sergeant Reid C. Chamberlain, who had been on Bataan and Corregidor early in the war with General MacArthur. Five hours after Corregidor fell, Chamberlain had escaped in a small boat and had made his way to Mindanao, where he had helped organize Filipino guerrilla bands. He had stayed there a year and a half. Eventually he had been taken out to Australia in a submarine, and had then returned to the United

States, where he had received the Distinguished Service Cross for "extraordinary heroism." Although he could have remained in the States for the rest of the war, he had asked for overseas duty again and had been sent to the 3d Division. Normally the rest of us would have dismissed as "crazy" the idea of a man volunteering to come back overseas, after what Chamberlain had done. Human beings don't go around asking for so much trouble. But Chamberlain was proof of some men's belief that, as long as the Axis was undefeated, a man could do no other than give his all to defeating it.

One day early in 1945, the rumors about our going into action again were confirmed. Our commanding officers told us that we were going on another operation as "floating reserve." We would not make the beachhead and might not have to land at all; it depended on how the battle went during the first day or two. Perhaps we would turn around and sail back without a fight. Then, probably, most of our men would be rotated home for a well-deserved furlough.

We drew combat gear and ammunition and again made our packs and rolls. Then we said goodbye once more to the members of our rear echelon—the men who would stay behind and take care of our possessions.

As we started off on the long hike to the docks, we were aware again of the naturalness and swiftness with which we moved toward battle. We passed the quartermaster tents and saw members of our rear echelon still sorting the equipment from the seabags of our casualties on Guam; they were cataloguing personal effects to send back to the dead and wounded men's kin. A few months hence they might be starting the process all over again. Some of us also recalled how our unit commanders had just managed to find time during the last week to award Purple Hearts and Bronze and Silver Stars for the Guam battle. And here we were taking off again. How many more months from now would our men be standing in long ranks to get more decorations—just before setting out for still another battle?

We wound across the hills and through the valleys where, months before, we had fought. We passed camp after camp of rear echelon units—Seabees, engineers, army and command outfits—and their men came down to the side of the road and watched us silently as we plodded by. We were in battle dress again—green dungarees, the old camouflaged helmet covers, combat packs and blanket rolls, weapons, knives, bayonets, canteens, first-aid kits, cigar boxes, paper-covered books—the same sort of things we had had with us when we had landed on Guam. The boys of the rear units, in their khaki and blue work clothes, smiled at us and called, "Get some Nips for us," and we imagined that under their breaths some of them were praying for us.

At the last moment I had been transferred from the 21st Marines to 3d Division headquarters to make more recordings. I was to be in a position to attach myself to the most favorable unit for that kind of work. It was assumed that General Erskine would accompany the first outfit of the Division to land. By staying near him, I would be in a better position than if I were on a ship with a rifle regiment that might not land until late in the campaign, if at all. The 21st Marines received a new combat correspondent, Corporal William J. Middlebrooks, who for two years had been a scout with Fox Company of the regiment. A veteran of Bougainville and Guam, Middlebrooks, who was twenty-three, had done some newspaper work in Florida before the war. The new assignment pleased him immensely; he could not foresee its tragic ending.

Ironically, we had no sooner boarded ships and set sail than the 21st Marines was ordered by the commanding general of the V Amphibious Corps, Lieutenant General Holland M. ("Howlin' Mad") Smith, to move out ahead and prepare to be the first unit of the 3d Division to land in the new operation. The rest of the 3d Division, including General Erskine's command ship to which I was assigned, was to come along behind. So, separated from my outfit which was now earmarked to go into battle first, I could do nothing but scowl at the men around me who told me I was lucky.

I didn't know how lucky I was.

Just before we had left Guam, some men of the 21st had been sitting around discussing the good luck of the Division in going to the new operation as "floating reserve." Our experience told us that the big casualties came from making the beachhead. As long as we didn't have to make the beachhead this time, we could consider ourselves fortunate.

"Yeah," said our first sergeant blackly. "But I don't like it. There's one thing wrong about luck: it runs out."

Soon after we set sail, our officers broke out the maps and overlays and showed us where we were going and the strength and nature of the enemy's defenses.

It was a small, volcanic, sandy island, five and a half miles long and two and a half miles wide at its widest point. It was shaped like a pork chop with a volcano on its southern, knoblike tip. There was nothing on its ugly, barren surface but three airfields and 23,000 Japs.

We were going to Iwo Jima.

IX

Back to Our Foxholes

IT IS problematical what an atomic bomb would have done to Iwo Jima. It might have made our invasion unnecessary. But in February 1945 we did not have the atomic bomb. For seventy-two days before our forces landed on Iwo, however, American planes and warships subjected that island to a continuous air and naval bombardment with the biggest bombs and shells we did have. It seemed inconceivable that anyone could live through the hell that rained almost without pause on the tiny plot of land. Beginning on December 8, 1944, Liberators, Superfortresses, night fighters, carrier bombers, and P-38s joined with the Fleet in hurling death and destruction on the Jap defenders. It wasn't much of a target— eight square miles. Our ships could reach every part of the island with their big guns. And our planes could pound it, yard by yard.

Yet, as the days went by prior to our invasion, the Japs seemed not only to hold their own beneath our bombings, but actually to become stronger. In December, long before we in the ranks had any idea that we might be going to Iwo, I spent several days at Saipan and visited Sergeant James J. McElroy, a combat correspondent attached to a Marine fighter unit based there. Each night McElroy was flying over the Bonins and the Volcanos with Marine night fighters.

"I don't understand it," he said ominously. "We're giving

153

Iwo Jima one of the worst drubbings you can imagine, and every night the ack-ack gets worse. Those Japs must be living underground."

McElroy was later lost over Iwo, shot down by the enemy ack-ack. But he was correct about the Japs: there were 23,000 of them on the island, living underground. Under their commander, Major General Tadamichi Kuribayashi, one of the ablest Jap leaders our troops had ever met, the enemy had made a solid fortress of Iwo. Firing positions, supply rooms, and living quarters were inside the ground, protected by layers of steel, concrete, and volcanic rock. The firing apertures and entrances were small, well hidden, and also protected by concrete and rock. There was very little above ground—a few supply buildings and pillboxes. These our planes and ships found and destroyed. But Iwo could not be leveled like a city. It was level already.

To many of us, studying the maps on our way to the island, Iwo looked like an eight-square-mile section taken out of the center of the most strongly fortified line in the world. Despite our inability to knock out the defenses, our reconnaissance planes photographed many of the Jap forts for us. Every yard on the island was covered by some kind of gun, and most of Iwo's sandy acreage seemed covered by a multitude of weapons that could catch us in all kinds of crossfire. The Jap strategy of defense seemed clear. There were only two possible landing beaches, one on the east side of the island and the other on the west. Both ran northward from the volcano, Mt. Suribachi, about thirty-five hundred yards. The rest of the coastline—circling the northern shore—was steep, jagged cliffs. The Japs would try to keep us off the beaches. Failing that, they would catch us on the flat open first airfield between the heights of Suribachi on the south and the high, rocky ridges in the north. They would shell us from both sides with their artillery, either annihilating us or driving us back into the sea.

It was a simple yet logical plan. The Jap artillery was

numerous, and it was big. There were 150 and 120 mm. rifles —siege-type guns, usually fired at long range. There were mortars up to the tremendous caliber of 320 millimeters. There were flat-trajectory weapons and heavy rocket bombs. All were zeroed-in not on a target several miles away, but on the open stretches of Iwo a few hundred yards directly in front of the firing positions. Moreover, the Jap guns occupied the high ground and were effectually hidden from sight. We would be caught on lower terrain without observation points and without cover. By contrast, most of the Jap defenders would fight from inside the ground, firing their weapons through tiny openings and cavelike entrances in the high ridges. Kuribayashi also had some infantry who would charge out at night in counterattacks if the big guns needed that kind of help. The 23,000 Japs were all the little island would hold, and it seemed that with such strong defenses this would be enough.

For many of us, the trip to Iwo was a tense one, even though we were "floating reserve." The way the island defenders had weathered our heavy bombardment and the indications of tremendous defenses pictured by the reconnaissance maps sobered us to a realization of the possibility that whoever did get ashore would be in for a rough fight.

As we moved northward, it became colder. We were used to the heat of the tropics, and we began to shiver. We wore shirts and dungaree blouses and heavy combat jackets over the blouses. At night the holds below the water level were cold. We undid our packs and slept in our clothes under blankets and ponchos. The pipes that carried cool air through the sleeping compartments gave us trouble. In the tropics men had punctured them in hundreds of places so that the refreshing breeze would blow onto the bunks on which the men were trying to sleep. But now we had to stuff the holes and prevent the air from blowing out on us and making us colder.

Early on D-day morning we went out on deck. We were still at sea far from Iwo. It was a cold, clear day. We stood about and shivered, waiting for news to come through the ship's loud-speakers.

"Gosh," one man said, "it's cold as winter."

"It *is* winter," a private retorted. "It's February 19, and we're out of the jungle, remember!"

Our ship, being Division command ship, had a lot of signal company men aboard. Their radios were to link the different elements of the outfit. The receivers began to crackle with the transmissions coming from Iwo. First we heard the conversations between the air observers and the units of the Fleet which were putting the finishing touches on the intensive shelling of the island. Then we heard the two-way conversations between units of the 4th and 5th Marine Divisions which were preparing to make the beachhead. The 4th Division were veterans of the Marshall Islands and Saipan and Tinian. The 5th Division was going into its first battle, although many of its men were veterans of other outfits that had seen action earlier in the war.

"Very light swells," a message crackled out. "Boating excellent. Visibility excellent."

We tightened and untightened our fists as we listened. Our hopes and prayers were for the men getting ready to land.

At 0849, eleven minutes before the first waves were to hit the beach, we heard: "No counterfire as yet. Beach obscured by smoke from our fire."

It sounded fine.

At 0852: "Few enemy mortar shells landing in water. Our boats moving in."

At 0900 the exciting news came: "First wave ashore."

Seven Marine battalions landed abreast on the 3500-yard-long eastern beach of Iwo. Enemy fire at first was light, a few scattered mortar shells and some machine-gun fire. We had "light" casualties. But the Japs were still stunned by our shelling. They didn't know whether this was our main landing or whether we would also suddenly thrust ashore on the western beaches. Our naval gunfire had lifted off the beaches as our men reached the sand and was now dropping five hundred yards inland along the base of the first airfield. Our men began climbing the steep, sandy slope to the field.

It was an arduous climb. The black volcanic sand offered poor footing. The men slid in it and left footprints like elephant tracks. The wind had formed a series of steep terraces on the slope, natural bunkers that held up our tanks and vehicles. Bulldozers cut paths through the bunkers, and tanks slowly got through. Our units moved ahead in platoon strength. Men moved cautiously, diving into bomb craters, pausing to see if any enemy were in the neighborhood, then advancing a few more yards. Behind them LSMs rammed against the beach and poured more tanks and vehicles ashore.

At 0930 we heard: "As yet no mines encountered. Receiving light small-arms fire and some artillery and mortar."

By 0956 one assault battalion had gone three hundred yards inland from the beach.

By 1000 all assault battalions were ashore. On shipboard, listening to the optimistic reports, we relaxed.

Then the Japs came to life.

From Mt. Suribachi, from the ridges and from all of northern Iwo, artillery and mortar shells crashed in a sudden storm. Machine guns opened fire from a host of pillboxes hidden in the sand dunes ahead of and around the men huddled on the beach. Twenty mm. dual-purpose guns fired down the beach point-blank from the heights of the airfield.

Our bombardment had prevented the Japs from keeping us from landing. Several thousand of our men had gotten ashore. Now the Japs prepared to annihilate those men and prevent anyone else from reaching the beach.

For a while it looked as if they might succeed. From ten in the morning until two in the afternoon no reinforcements got ashore. A few small boats braved the storm of Jap shells to rush in urgently needed ammunition. But to all intents and purposes, the men already on the beach were cut off.

The steep slopes in which the assault troops tried to dig

became death traps. The heavy Jap shells landed among the huddling masses of men with increasing frequency. The wounds were ghastly. The big enemy missiles mangled the men beyond recognition. The ground shook crazily from the explosions; it was as if a man were lying on a bouncing beach. Men pushed into the sand and hung on. The crashes beat against their heads and gave them concussion. The roar grew greater; the sand flew like hail; the air became smoky and unreal. Everything seemed to rock and spin.

Some units tried to push ahead. But now the Japs were on the beach. Having weathered our bombardment in dugouts and bombproofs beneath the dunes, they reappeared at firing holes with rifles, hand grenades, and machine guns. Some of the enemy blockhouses and pillboxes under the dunes had been partly destroyed, but there were still Japs in them, alive and fighting back.

One of our units that tried to push forward was led by "Manila John" Basilone, who had won the Congressional Medal of Honor on Guadalcanal. After he won the Medal, Basilone could have stayed in the United States. But he wanted to continue fighting with a good machine-gun outfit, so he went overseas again as a Gunnery Sergeant. In the midst of the Jap hail of fire, he urged his men up the Iwo slope. He was out in front, near the airfield, when a Jap shell burst. It killed him instantly.

Somehow, in all the fire, small units of men made progress. The fearless bravery and devotion to duty of the individual men and the teams of men who eventually won the victory on Iwo was at no time more outstanding than on D-day. Uncommon valor, as Admiral Nimitz later said, was a common virtue. It held the beachhead for us.

By two in the afternoon Jap fire had slackened enough for reserves to come in. The men who had held and deepened the beachhead looked back to the most encouraging sight of the day. Wave after wave of reinforcements were hurtling onto the sand. Jap fire was still heavy, and it continued heavy all the rest of that day. But the men went on pushing inland, and by the end of D-day a unit of the 5th Division reached the other side of the island to cut off Mt. Suribachi from the rest of Iwo.

That night those of us out on ship, who had been following the course of the battle by radio, were sure that the Japs would launch a banzai charge against the men ashore. It seemed inevitable that the enemy would use the night to try to hurl us off the island by an infantry attack.

There were no reports during the night. It was as though the island were shrouded in silence. We imagined our men lying tensely in foxholes, listening and waiting.

In the morning, however, we learned that there had been a Jap night attack. A battalion of enemy infantry had raced down the runway of the first airfield to hit the unit in the center of our lines. Our men had been ready. They called for illumination shells and mowed the Japs down by the light. Kuribayashi failed again. Perhaps if it had been a stronger, all-out attack, it would have succeeded. When dawn of D plus 1 came, however, our men were in a position to continue their attack.

Throughout the second day we continued to listen to the radios. We heard our aerial observers in little "grasshopper" observation planes reporting the positions of our men, and we plotted the positions on a big map that we had on deck.

" I see some Marines in the lower left-hand corner of target area 192 Able," we would hear one of the observers say. We would look at the map and see that that was an advance of about fifty yards from where Marines had last been seen.

Most of the day the news looked good. Our men were crossing the first airfield in strength. The line was drawing tighter around the base of Suribachi. Movement was beginning to be made northward toward the second airfield.

"They won't need us," one of our men said. "This thing will be over in five days."

We cruised around in the open sea and began to play cards

and read magazines. Some members of the 3d Division band who were aboard had brought their instruments, and in one of the holds three of them played some classical pieces. A truck driver, lying on his sack, groaned. "Can't you give with some boogie?" he asked.

The band members paid no attention to him but continued with their classical numbers. Then they started a game: they played melodies from symphonies, and the men tried to guess what they were playing. Half the men had never before heard either the pieces or the names of the composers, but they liked the melodies. One of the bandsmen played some Tchaikovsky. "Christ!" a BARman exclaimed. "That's the *Moon Song*. Tommy Dorsey, ain't it?"

In the afternoon the progress of the battle didn't look so good. In some places our lines were going back; in others, there had been no progress. Several observation planes had been shot down. Their pilots had disappeared among the rocks and mysterious wastes of Jap-held territory.

Then we heard about our casualties.

They shocked us. They ranged from 25 to 35 percent among the assault units. Several thousand men had already been evacuated. An average of three men were being hit every minute. In the evening ominous word reached our ship: The 4th and 5th Divisions needed reinforcements, and the 21st Marines were going to be ordered in.

It was three days before we found out what happened to my regiment after it got ashore. During those three days we tried to follow its progress by radio. The symbols on our map showed that it relieved a regiment of the 4th Division in the center of the line that was pushing northward. It was in an area lying between the first and second airfields. For two days it made almost no progress. We heard that the battle was desperate, that a crisis was reached, that the Japs had stopped us and were inflicting heavy casualties on us. We thought of all our friends on shore and tried to imagine the hell through which they must be living. Most of those days it was cold and gray and rainy, which must have made the men in the sandy foxholes miserable. Even the news that Suribachi had been scaled and taken failed to cheer us. Now we had the highest ground on the island. The Japs could no longer shoot down on our backs as we pushed northward. But this seemed of slight importance as we saw the positions of the 21st remaining the same hour after hour. We wanted to know what was happening. When we did find out, later, the story was simple but heartrending, especially to those of us who had had friends in the regiment.

This was the story:

The 21st, after going ashore, had been ordered to pierce a belt of Jap underground pillboxes, bunkers, and bombproofs, most of which had withstood our pre-invasion naval and aerial bombardment. The enemy forts faced in all directions and were filled with Jap machine gunners and riflemen. To attack them, our men had to cross exposed sandy stretches. When the Marines rose up to charge, they had been subjected to a withering fire, not only from the forts immediately in front of them, but from the bigger enemy guns and mortars looking down on the area from the ridges in the central part of Iwo.

During the first two days of this assault, the 1st and 2nd battalions of the 21st lost almost 50 percent of their men. Gains were negligible. Units were pinned down in the sand and kept there. On the third day, the 3d battalion of the 21st went into the lines for the first time with orders to pierce the Jap defenses at all costs. Our situation by then had become critical. We could not remain much longer sitting in the open, suffering casualties. And there was no room for end plays around the Jap forts. The 3d battalion had to go through.

Behind a heavy bombardment, I and K Companies of the battalion launched the attack. With bayonets fixed, the fresh troops crept slowly forward. Jap fire picked up, as it had on the two previous days. Machine-gun and rifle bullets zipped through the air. A few men fell, but the others kept going.

More and more mortar shells crashed among them. Captain Rockmore urged on his Company I: Keep going! He directed them at a row of Jap pillboxes. An enemy bullet struck him in the throat, killing him instantly. A moment later three of his lieutenants went down. Sergeants took over the platoons, and the men kept going, faster and faster. The commanding officer of K Company fell. First Lieutenant Raoul Archambault, one of the bravest and most-decorated men in the 3d Division, took over and rushed the outfit forward.

Heaving grenades, stumbling over the sand, refusing to let the intense Jap fire pin them down, the men poured ahead. They reached a line of pillboxes, jabbed with their bayonets at wildly moving Jap forms, dropped grenades into holes and behind rocks, and hurtled up and over the first line of forts. Their charge became a rush as they surged past mounds of pillboxes and up the slope leading to the second airfield.

Behind them, our mortar men gave them enthusiastic support. Sixties and 81s shot high through the air over the heads of the advancing troops. Our tanks, long held up, began to grind ahead. The Japs answered with furious fire from their positions north of the airfield. Enemy missiles from antitank guns, 120 mm. rifles, 320 mm. mortars, bazooka-type rocket throwers, and 75 mm. howitzers were hurled at the charging green-dungareed troops. Still, Companies I and K swept on, past pillboxes and through minefields. In a wild burst they flowed suddenly onto·the second airfield and raced across it to a fifty-foot ridge on the opposite side of the strip.

Archambault's outfit was the first across. After a moment's pause at the base of the ridge to reorganize a platoon, he led it up the ridge. The rocky hill was filled with Jap pillboxes connected by fire trenches. Our men used grenades and bayonets in a hand-to-hand struggle. The Japs drove them down in a counterattack. Our men again reformed. Archambault, who had won medals on Bougainville and Guam for gallantry in action, was surpassing any of his previous moments of bravery. Once more he led his men up the ridge. The Marines stood together as the Japs rushed from their holes to drive them down again. A sergeant in a hand-to-hand struggle with a snarling, hissing Jap officer was attacked by a second Jap. A Marine corporal shot the second Jap, then helped the sergeant finish the enemy officer. Two Marines were rushed by five Japs. The Marines fought back-to-back until other Marines could help them. The battle was brief and bloody. When it was over, the 3d battalion was on top of the ridge, eight hundred yards out from where it had begun its attack ninety minutes before. Through the hole punched in the Jap line, our whole attack now poured. Tanks, bazooka men, mortars, and machine gunners streamed through the mine-fields and rows of pillboxes, attacking the by-passed Jap forts, and wiping them out one by one.

On the left flank, the 2nd battalion also moved forward that day. Free at last from some of the flanking fire that had pinned it down, the outfit moved out of their field of death and reached the southern apron of the second airfield.

What had been accomplished was realized when mopping-up parties discovered more than eight hundred individual, mutually supporting Jap pillboxes and blockhouses in an area one thousand yards long and two hundred yards deep, protecting the second airfield. That was what had held up our men of the 21st for two days. It was what with bayonet and hand grenades our men had finally smashed through in a desperate ninety-minute charge.

That same day (D plus 5) those of us who were still out on the Division command ship miles from Iwo were told that we were going to land. The 9th Marines were also ordered ashore. The 21st Marines needed a rest; the 9th would replace them.

We sailed through the night and at dawn were off Iwo. The little island looked, as one man said, like a half-submerged mummy case. A tiny American flag flew from the heights of

Suribachi. The northern half of the island, which was higher than the area of the landing beaches, was covered with brown and yellow smoke. Every so often we could see a bright red flash. A vast array of ships of every description ringed the island. Battleships, cruisers, and destroyers were standing close in, firing at targets on the island. LSTs, LSMs, LCIs, and other green-painted amphibious craft moved among the larger ships, making their way to the beach to land supplies, or backing out after having taken on casualties. Big blue transports and cargo vessels rocked silently in the water, unloading supplies into the amphibious craft. Near the beach, so close that it seemed to be almost on the sand, was a white hospital ship. A group of brown Ducks—amphibious trucks —rolled in the water by its side, unloading men on stretchers. The casualties were lifted by a winch and lines.

Altogether there were more than eight hundred ships engaged in the work of taking this little island.

Our first job was to unload ammunition. Our artillery and mortars were running short on the beach, and our holds were filled with the precious shells. We didn't know it then, but our artillery was engaged in a stirring up-hill fight against seemingly overwhelming odds. The big guns had been going in ever since D-day. They had set up on the exposed slopes at the sides of the first airfield and on the low ground near the base of Suribachi. The Japs could look down on them and cover them with fire from their high positions. Our observers had to look upwards to find targets, and our gunners had to fire upwards. In clear weather our observation planes helped to locate the targets, but it had been raining most of the time so that the burden had fallen on ground forward observers. These FOs had suffered many casualties, trying to spot Jap targets. Even when they found them, it was frequently impossible for our gunners to knock out the enemy positions. The Jap guns were so well emplaced that often a direct hit into a small hole was necessary to silence the enemy's piece.

All day we unloaded ammunition. Our bandsmen worked in the holds, filling the cargo nets with clover leaves of shells and crates of high explosives. On Guam the bandsmen had been litter-bearers, but they had suffered so many casualties that on this operation it was decided that they would help unload the ships and, if landed, act as Division CP security personnel.

In the evening we had an air raid. We knew that a screen of carriers and warships was between us and Japan, guarding our operation against interference from enemy ships or planes. Units in that screen were several times attacked by Jap kamikaze flyers. The *Saratoga* was hit but retired from the scene under her own power. Later the *Bismarck Sea* was sunk. These ships were out of sight from us, and we had no idea of actions that were occurring. We put our faith in our Fleet's ability to protect us, and we were not disappointed. Only three times were Jap planes able to get past our task force, and only twice were they able to drop bombs around Iwo. This night was one of those times.

Our ships put up a smoke screen that blotted us out from one another and from aerial observers; we seemed to be in a thick fog. We heard planes over us, and soon we heard ackack and explosions. Our bandsmen and the other men unloading the ship had to pause. The little boats around us, taking on the ammunition, could not move. Some of us were on deck, wrapped in the thick smoke. Something hissed through the fog near us. There was a crash in the water, and pieces of metal spattered against the steel sides of the ship. A red flame burned in the water a few feet near us.

One of our men on deck walked calmly past us. He was holding on to his leg. His dungaree trousers were torn, and blood was oozing down his knee. He laughed. "Does this rate a Purple Heart?" he asked.

He was the only man hit, although fragments continued to splash around us for another half hour. As it was, we didn't know whether he had been hurt by fragments from an enemy bomb or from some of our own ack-ack. But it was our first casualty. We were in the battle.

We continued unloading that night, and the next day received orders to land.

It was a bright, clear day. The air was cold. We went over the side, down the cargo net, and into an LCM. The coxswain by now was a veteran. He had been taking men in since D-day. His face was unshaven, and his eyes were watery. He had been sleeping on a cot in the well of his LCM. He looked at us patronizingly as if he considered us boots.

"What are you?" he said to us. "The garrison?"

We didn't answer.

On the way in, a mortar shell landed about twenty feet from our boat, making a sudden, sharp crash in the water, and a white fountain sent spray over us. We ducked, and the coxswain laughed.

"I thought the battle was over," a sergeant said to him.

"It is," the coxswain answered. "That's just some fanatic that won't give up."

We were guided toward shore by a series of control boats —small ships that stayed in radio contact with the beach-masters on the various beaches, telling them what was coming in and asking for permission to land whoever wanted to be landed. The control ships passed us forward from one to another. "Go in about two thousand yards and report to number 652," one ship told us.

We moved in the two thousand yards and reported to boat number 652. He asked us who we were and what we were carrying and told us to wait. In a little while he flagged us on. "Move in about five hundred yards and about fifteen hundred yards up the beach and report to number 79," he called through a megaphone.

We reported to boat 79 and gradually drew nearer to the beach. We could see great confusion on the sand—piles of equipment of all kinds, wrecked boats and vehicles, casualty evacuation stations, dugouts and foxholes, tanks and amtracs and artillery firing positions. Men seemed to be living and working on top of each other. The entire slope leading up to the airfield was covered with men and equipment, units so interspersed that it was almost impossible to find any one particular outfit. Placards and signs waved in the breeze, indicating the code names for the various beaches, the location of communications and message centers, and the directions to aid stations and command units. From the midst of the confused mass, our guns were firing, dug into the sand with only their muzzles pointing above ground. Occasionally a Jap mortar shell burst somewhere on the slope, and everyone dove into the sand. Then we would see a team of litter bearers scrambling up the hill toward where the black smoke of the burst still billowed.

The air over the water was filled with the familiar smell of blood and death. Pale white bodies still floated in the water, face down, some of them bobbing among torn lifejackets. Just as we received orders to land, a body without a head bumped lightly against the side of our ship; we stared at it with sickened horror. The next instant our coxswain gunned the motor and we shot up on the black sand.

We marched slowly up the slope that led to the airfield. It was the same route taken by the men who had had to fight their way up on D-day: a long, hard climb in the sliding sand. The entire slope was pocked by huge shell craters in which men were living and working—unloaders, rear elements, and artillerymen. We passed a unit of Negro Army Duck drivers who had been on the island since D-day, landing ammunition in their Ducks and taking out wounded; they were still doing this work. Their foxholes were covered by shelterhalves and ponchos. Empty ration boxes and cans were strewn around. The men, haggard and tired, watched us silently as we marched past them.

Near the top of the slope a sign on a piece of cardboard pointed north with an arrow: "The Front." We turned northward and in single file moved along the edge of the airfield.

Battered Jap planes were piled along the top of the slope, the wreckage gleaming in the sun. A handful of men with carbines over their shoulders climbed among the wreckage, looking for hunks of aluminum for souvenir watchstraps. Nearby a sign said: "Danger. Booby traps."

As we reached the northern end of the field a mortar shell landed near us, and was followed by another. We broke into a trot and hurried toward the protection of a sandy slope marking the field's northern boundary. A green banner with yellow letters was stuck in the ground: "21st CP." I hurried faster, through a line of weasels (amphibious cars) and jeeps, to a mass of men who were sitting and lying on the sand. The faces were all familiar, yet unfamiliar. They were men I had seen a week ago, but it suddenly seemed as if I hadn't seen them for ten years. They were bearded and hunched over. Their clothes were dirty and torn; their eyes watery and distant; their hair matted; their lips puffed and black, and their mouths were open as if they were having trouble breathing.

One man came over to me and took both of my hands in his. He stared through me, looking as if he had been crying.

"We did it," he said. "We broke through."

He belonged to one of the rifle companies. I wondered what he was doing back at the CP.

"They want to evacuate me," he said. "I got hit twice."

I noticed a bandage on his wrist and some white under a slashed pants leg.

Jerry Gruggen, the ambulance driver in our outfit, came over. He was dirty and tired, his eyes were bloodshot, and he was quivering. He seemed mad.

"Come on," he said to the rifleman. "You want to go down to the beach, or don't you?"

"I don't," the rifleman said.

Gruggen took his arm impatiently. "Come on," he said. "You don't know what you're doing." He hustled him over to the ambulance. "Get the hell in before I hit you."

The rifleman stumbled into the rear of the ambulance and sat down. There were two stretcher cases already in the ambulance. Gruggen noticed me as he climbed into the driver's seat. For an instant he smiled.

"They took us out of the lines," he said disgustedly. "It was about time. A little bit more, and there wouldn't have been any of us left."

I walked among the men and felt ashamed of my clean clothes. They nodded and waved at me, and some of them called out wearily to ask where I had been. The whole regiment was in reserve. The men had dug in, but most of them seemed too groggy and dazed to fall asleep. It was as if they were afraid something else might happen to them if they relaxed their guard and closed their eyes.

At the top of the slope, in a row of abandoned Jap pillboxes and bombproofs, I found my company and most of my friends. They all seemed dazed and grim. Our first sergeant was living in a particularly luxurious pillbox that had served as a Jap sickbay. The fort had concrete and rock walls fourteen feet thick and was completely covered by volcanic sand. To enter, one had to squeeze into a tiny opening below the level of the surrounding ground and push along a narrow passageway. Inside were cots, upholstered chairs, and tables. The Japs had had magazines, phonograph records, and other comforts to help pass the time during our bombardments. Some of the bombproofs in the vicinity also had electric lights and running water. They were incongruous retreats amid all the desolation in the area. In another, I found my friend Walter Page, who had been on the ambush on Guam with me, and one of our combat correspondents, Sergeant Dick Dashiell. Both men were bleary-eyed and tense from the fighting of the last three days. Dashiell held a sheaf of typewritten papers—stories that had been written by our new combat correspondent, Bill Middlebrooks, the young scout from Florida.

Dashiell rolled his tongue around in his cheek thoughtfully.

"Middlebrooks is dead," he said. "He was carrying ammunition. Got shot in the back by a sniper."

I sat down in the bombproof.

"He's not the only guy," Page said bitterly. "After two years overseas—after going through Bougainville and Guam —we run into something like this." He began reeling off names. "Captain Rockmore's dead. Captain Kirby's dead. Colonel Williams is wounded. Major Murray's wounded. Captain Cousins got a leg blown off. B Company's cut to pieces. All those guys who lived through the banzai attack on Guam are either dead or wounded. We've got only three company commanders left in the whole regiment."

I picked up a piece of paper that one of our men at the foot of the hill had handed to me as a possible story to write. It was a translation of a mimeographed sheet in Japanese that our men had found posted on gun pits and inside the dugouts. It was entitled "Courageous Battle Vow," and read:

"1. Above all else we will dedicate ourselves and our entire strength to the defense of this island.

"2. We will grasp bombs, charge the enemy tanks, and destroy them.

"3. We will infiltrate into the midst of the enemy and annihilate them.

"4. With every salvo we will, without fail, kill the enemy.

"5. Each man will make it his duty to kill ten of the enemy before dying.

"6. Until we are destroyed to the last man we will harass the enemy by guerrilla tactics."

I laid the paper down. "Looks as if the Japs were living up to their vows," I said.

Page snorted. "Stick around," he said. "It's only the beginning."

X

"How Do You Stay Alive?"

THE DAY after I came ashore I joined the 1st battalion of the 21st. Jerry Gruggen drove me to the battalion's aid station in his jeep ambulance. To many of the Marines, Gruggen and the other ambulance drivers were the unsung heroes of our battles. They raced back and forth all day long and most of the night, taking casualties from the front-line aid stations to the beach evacuation stations. The ambulances were usually the first vehicles to follow the front-line troops into new territory. They had to keep up with the infantry and the forward aid stations. That meant that they frequently had to do the pioneering work in finding roads and trails to the front. They went through territory still held by the enemy, and often they hit mines, because they went over roads before engineers had a chance to find the mines.

Combat correspondents, who had to move around quickly from outfit to outfit, found the jeep ambulances the best means of conveyance. The drivers knew the latest positions of the front-line units and could take us speedily wherever we wanted to go. They were also up on the latest news in each outfit. They took out the wounded, and they knew who died. They picked up gossip and stories from every outfit they worked with, and they knew who the men's heroes were and who had accomplished what.

The 1st battalion aid station nestled in a revetment at the northern end of one of the runways of the first airfield. The black sand revetment was about fifteen feet high, and the corpsmen were dug into the sand banks. They were administering dressings and plasma to several wounded men who lay in the sandy holes. The unit, under the command of Dr. Charles A. Jost, was supposedly in reserve, as was the whole battalion. But the doctors and corpsmen were as busy as if they were still in the front lines.

"Trouble is," one of the corpsmen said tiredly, "there's no place to rest on this island. Everywhere is the front."

A few minutes earlier, a stream of Jap mortar shells had landed on top of the revetment. Fragments had showered down on the men, wounding several. They were lying silently, with curious peaceful smiles on their faces, waiting to be helped into Gruggen's ambulance. They looked as if they knew they were through with Iwo.

Just after we arrived, a sudden commotion broke out on top of the revetment. Two men were standing there against the skyline. One of the doctors yelled at them: "Get the hell down. You want to draw fire?"

But the men ignored him. Then several other men appeared. The doctor began to scramble up the steep wall, muttering angrily, his face red. Suddenly there was a terrific blast on top of the revetment, and a shower of sand flew into the air. It was followed by another blast. The doctor tumbled down the slope and flung himself into a hole, swearing at the top of his lungs. The corpsmen and wounded clung to the side of the revetment, seeking shelter from another blast. After a moment, the men relaxed. Gruggen picked himself up from where he had sought safety and went over to his ambulance. He examined it quickly to see whether any fragments had hit it. The doctor who had fallen down the slope looked up bitterly. His face was covered with sand. "Damn fools," he muttered.

IWO PILLBOX. The Marines at the right are "buttoning up" the Japs in the pillbox. In a moment the flamethrower in the center will go to work.

OVER A RIDGE. Beneath the tumbled rocks on the ridge are caverns and tunnels still filled by Japs. Rear units will have to dig them out.

There was a short, sharp scream from the top of the revetment, and a voice called weakly, "Help!"

The doctor and several corpsmen grabbed first-aid pouches and scrambled up the revetment. A moment later one of the corpsmen looked down and called for more men.

"There's a whole bunch of guys been hit up here," he shouted. "Bring up some stretchers."

Three more corpsmen struggled up the steep slope, dragging litters and first-aid kits. On top of the revetment the ground sloped away to a small tableland, covered with the shattered remains of stunted banyan trees. The two Jap shells had hit among a group of men who had been digging into the area. Torn, charred equipment lay among the blasted tree roots. A pile of helmets and shovels were punched with holes. Twelve men were lying on the ground, bleeding onto the black sand, three of them dead, the other nine wounded.

The corpsmen went to work, tying on combat dressings and giving plasma. Most of the wounded were writhing with pain. They rubbed their hands across their foreheads and groaned. One man who had been hit in the leg felt better than the others and was talkative. The doctor was dressing his leg. Every so often the doctor looked around angrily and cautioned the corpsmen to stay down.

"Did anybody escape?" the man with the wounded leg asked.

The doctor shook his head. "You sure asked for it," he said. "What the hell were you doing up here?"

"This was an artillery observation team," the wounded man said. "How can you see the Japs on this damn island if you don't stick your head up?"

The doctor didn't answer.

Slowly, the wounded men were lowered down the wall of the revetment. Gruggen took them back to the beach. A corpsman made a note of the names, ranks, and serial numbers of the men who had been evacuated. His hand was trembling, and his nose was running. He could hardly write; it seemed as if his fingers were numb from cold, and his writing looked like the jerky scrawl of a drunken man.

As he was finishing, a loud, rumbling noise approached the revetment along the open airstrip. Dr. Jost sprang to his feet and ran to the revetment's opening. A halftrack was moving along the runway, trying to stay close to the shelter of the line of embankments. Dr. Jost waved at it angrily. He cupped his hands over his mouth and shouted at the driver to stay away from the revetment. One of the corpsmen instinctively huddled against the wall of his foxhole.

"Good God!" he breathed.

The next instant, so foreseeable that not a person was shocked by it, there was a burst of earth beneath the halftrack, followed by a sharp crash. The vehicle rose slowly and turned over, settling in a cloud of dust and sand. Dr. Jost threw himself flat as debris rained through the air. The corpsmen ducked their heads and laughed hysterically at each other. What had happened seemed as inexorable as a Greek tragedy.

When the dust settled, Dr. Jost and two corpsmen raced into the open to the smoking halftrack. Five burned bodies lay among the twisted wreckage. The corpsmen extricated them and dragged them into the revetment. A mortar shell fell on the airstrip near the wrecked halftrack, and a Jap Nambu machine gun opened fire from the rocks north of the runway.

"The halftrack hit something big," one of the corpsmen said, out of breath. "Must have been a torpedo warhead."

Three of the halftrack crew were already dead. Two were still alive. Again the corpsmen went to work with bandages and plasma. The man with the book examined the wounded Marines' dog tags for their names and serial numbers. One of the injured men had his dog tags tied to the laces of his shoes, rather than around his neck. The corpsman lifted the wounded man's foot tenderly and copied the statistics. A few minutes later another jeep ambulance arrived to take out the two men.

One of the corpsmen turned to Doctor Jost. "Well," he said, rubbing his dust-streaked face, "who's next?"

Gruggen came back to the aid station with two sailors in his ambulance.

"What are the swabbies doing here?" one of the corpsmen exclaimed.

Gruggen laughed. "They want to kill some Japs. I told them I'd give them a lift this far."

No one at the aid station thought it was funny. The sailors were in blue dungarees, with dirty white sailor caps, and had carbines over their shoulders. They seemed embarrassed.

"We're working down on the beach," one of them said. "Thought we could find some souvenirs."

"Go on, beat it, swabbies!" one of the corpsmen said angrily.

"Okay, okay," the sailor answered. He paused and smiled. "How do you stay alive on this island anyway?"

"It's luck," Gruggen said. "If Lady Luck is on your side, you stay alive. If not—" He made a motion of kissing the air with his fingers.

The sailors nodded embarrassedly and shuffled out of the revetment. They paused on the airstrip, looking at the smoking ruins of the halftrack. Then they looked around, as if trying to decide whether to go back to the beach or head for the front. They turned slowly and trudged toward the front.

Later their bodies were brought back to our cemetery. No one saw them die.

I left the aid station and made my way to the 1st battalion's companies. I moved forward beneath the protection of the wall of revetments lining the runway. In one revetment I came on a big-shouldered mortarman. He was excited and shaking and could scarcely talk. He was standing over a pile of 10-in-1 ration boxes beside a wrecked Jap plane. An M-1 rifle was over his shoulder.

"Look," he blurted, grabbing my arm. He pointed to an

unexploded Jap 75 mm. shell, lying about five feet from the ration boxes. The nose of the shell was dug into the ground.

The mortarman motioned at himself. "I'm here guarding these rations," he said. "They're for the companies—up there," he pointed up the embankment. "I'm standing here when—*whoosh*—this thing comes right over my shoulder, skids across the pile of rations, and plops into the ground. I saw it—but I couldn't do anything. I stand here staring— like it's gonna go off in my face. But it don't! It's a dud!" He laughed loudly and gripped my shoulder. "How do you like that? A dud!"

We had a smoke, and he calmed down. I asked him where the companies were. He motioned up the embankment again.

"About two hundred yards ahead, dug into some bushes and sand dunes. But you gotta be careful. You gotta cross an open field. They been throwing mortars up there."

I tried to stall climbing the embankment. If I had known the terrain and what lay up there, I would have felt differently. But making the first venture into country I hadn't seen held the terrors of facing the unknown. Finally I chucked my cigarette away and climbed the embankment. The ground above looked like a desert of black sand. The field was pocked with large shellholes. About two hundred yards across the field the sand rose in precipitous dunes covered with scraggly bushes and torn banyan trees. The dunes covered one of the rows of Jap pillboxes that had been pierced by the 3d battalion's charge. Dead Marines lay in awkward positions on the ground where they had fallen during the charge. Their faces were purple and puffed, and their weapons were rusty and full of sand.

I loped across the field, zigzagging and keeping low. I heard the sharp, clear dat-dat-dat-dat of a Nambu. Halfway across, I passed a Marine running the other way. It was Reid Chamberlain, the sergeant who had come overseas after having been with the guerrillas in the Philippines. He was a runner with the 1st battalion. He was hanging onto his helmet, trying to keep it from bouncing off his head. There was a nonchalant grin on his face, as if to indicate that he had been through worse experiences.

Able (A) and Baker (B) Companies were dug into foxholes among the sand dunes and bushes across the field. The foxholes were close together around a knocked-out Jap antitank gun that poked through a concrete fort built between two dunes. The men looked as if they had just come out of a hard-fought football game. They leaned against the sides of their foxholes, exhausted and breathing heavily. Their eyes were wide open and staring, as if they could not forget the terrible sights they had seen. I recognized many friends and tried talking to them, but it was useless: They looked through me, their answers made no sense, their minds wandered. One man tried to ask me how the battle was going. He couldn't get his question out. He finished half the sentence, then repeated the last words, over and over, like a man falling asleep. But he wasn't drowsing; his mind just wouldn't function.

A sergeant crawled over and smiled good-naturedly. He stared at me a moment as though he were going to cry. Then he wiped his nose.

"Any—any mail—yet?"

I shook my head. A little later, when I was with another unit, I heard that the sergeant was killed. He was one of the best-liked men in his outfit. The man who told me that he was dead said simply: "There goes the heart of this company."

Able Company had one officer left—a captain, and he kept rubbing his hand over his face as he sat in his foxhole.

"We're in reserve," he said. "But we're still losing men. We had two fellows hit by a mortar just a little while ago. Both good men. As good as they come." He stared into space, dreaming.

A few minutes later a lieutenant and four enlisted men slid over one of the sand dunes from our rear. They had carbines and rifles and were dragging stretchers. I recognized them. They were from the 3d battalion.

The lieutenant smiled half-heartedly at the captain.

"We're picking up our dead," he said. Then he added, "I hear we're going into the lines again this afternoon."

The captain nodded.

The lieutenant sighed and motioned the enlisted men to follow him. They picked their way cautiously across the clearing to the bodies that sprawled on the sand. The Nambu opened fire again. The men stooped over, ignoring the machine gun. When they reached the bodies, they rolled them onto the stretchers and took them back to the safety of the revetment. They had to make several trips to pick up all the bodies.

That afternoon the 1st and 3d battalions prepared to go back into the lines. By evening the order hadn't come, however, and the men dug in again for the night. No one knew the situation at the front or why the battalions hadn't moved or where they would go, if and when they did move. But no one cared; somebody else could worry about all that—somebody who was running the operation. To the men in the foxholes it was another evening alive.

The night in the sand was hideous. Land crabs crawled among the bushes and down the dunes, scraping along the ashes and sounding like Japs slithering toward our foxholes. Illumination flares hung overhead, casting weird, moving shadows across the terrain. The Japs threw mortar shells, and our artillery answered, and the sky was filled with the whirring breath of missiles sailing back and forth above our heads. Every so often a terrific crash sounded close by, where a mortar shell fell among us. We dozed in turns, trying to ignore the clamor, which in our fitful dreams sounded like someone banging doors in a house in which we were trying to sleep. The doors were all around us, upstairs and downstairs, in the same room and on the other side of the house. Suddenly someone slammed a door in our face. We awoke with a start. The banging was still going on. Sand was caving in on us from the lip of the foxhole. It was in our mouth and our ears. We shifted our position and tried to sleep again. The man guarding our foxhole didn't notice our stirring. He lay silently against the edge of the foxhole, staring into the night.

The next morning before dawn the order came to move up. The 9th Marines had made gains during the two days they had pressed the attack, but they were worn out and they needed support. The 3d battalion of the 21st passed us in a line, going to the northern end of the second airfield to attack the Japs in the high ground of the center of Iwo. The men trudged silently across the dunes and past the smashed Jap pillboxes. Their rifles were on their shoulders with bayonets already fixed. Machine gunners carried the sections of their guns, leaning forward beneath their heavy metal loads. Men carrying boxes of ammunition walked beside them, quiet and businesslike; one tobacco-chewing youth spat every few yards. After the machine gunners came the mortar men with their weapons. The line paused, and one of the men nodded at me. I hardly recognized him, with his black, scraggly beard and the rings of caked sand around his eyes.

"Where are we going?" he said anxiously.

Someone ahead of him turned around. "What do you care? You'll get there."

The line shoved off again. Garron, the little automatic rifleman who had killed the five Japs in the Guam jungle, walked by. "Isn't this a hell of a piece of real estate?" he called.

When the 1st battalion moved, it climbed through the rows of pillboxes, crossed the southern end of the second airfield, and went into position to the left of the 3d battalion. Here the terrain changed. The volcanic sand dunes were left behind. Instead, our men faced a wild, barren stretch of rocky ridges, cut into crags, chasms, and gulleys. It looked like the Bad Lands of the American West—or, as someone said, like hell with the fire out.

Our attack began early in the morning, following the first rolling barrage of the campaign. The shellfire ahead of our lines was thunderous. Our men squirmed into the ground and kept their heads down. The uninterrupted crashing of fire among the Jap positions made us wonder how any enemy could remain alive. For forty-nine minutes, 75, 105, and 155 mm. ground artillery shells and 5-, 6-, and 8-inch naval shells smashed among the ridges where the Japs were hiding. Then, on a time signal, the barrage lifted and moved ahead to crash down on Jap positions one hundred yards farther out. At the same time our men rose from their holes and began the attack. The riflemen, with fixed bayonets, and hand grenades hanging from their belts, ran toward the rocks. On the left the 1st battalion moved two hundred yards before the stunned Japs could recover. Then, when enemy mortar shells began falling again and bullets hit among our men, the Marines paused and sought cover. Slowly they broke into teams, and one by one rose again to attack the individual Jap positions, now all around them.

PFCs with smoke bombs and phosphorous grenades clambered among the rocks to within throwing distance of the Jap holes. As soon as they had hurled their grenades, and great puffs of smoke blanketed the walls of the ridge, flame-throwers came forward, running as fast as they could across the open. It seemed unbelievable that they could move as quickly as they did under their seventy-two-pound apparatus. Automatic riflemen and bazooka men moved up to cover the flame-throwers. The smoke drifted away from the ridge wall and cave openings were revealed, like huge black teeth in an ogre's face. As the riflemen watched each hole, the flame-thrower, completely exposed, shot his burning liquid into the cave, then turned and ran behind the protection of rocks. Other men took his place, heaving grenades or firing their bazookas, to finish the job.

Sometimes the men were pinned down among the rocks by flanking fire from other Jap positions. Sometimes the flame and bazookas and grenades didn't do the job, and tanks were called up to fire point-blank into the caves; flame-throwing tanks also took a hand. Knocked-out positions often came back to life; the Japs merely retreated into the underground tunnels, went to other holes, and then returned hours later to the cave that supposedly had been burned out.

On that day of the first rolling barrage we lost many men before we were finally stopped. Behind us by nightfall were many rocky ridges and hills covered with bodies of dead Marines. One of those ridges had been the scene of a particularly wild battle. Our men had charged to the top, using grenades and bayonets, and had engaged in a bloody hand-to-hand fight with Japs who had chosen to come out of their holes. There had been 150 mm. gun-pits on top of the ridge. The guns had been wrecked by our bombardments, and their torn, pocked barrels pointed starkly into the sky. But from the pits, entrance-ways led underground into the bowels of the ridge. Through those entrance-ways the Japs had surged to meet our charge. Our men caught them with their bayonets, clubbed them with butt strokes, threw grenades at them, and fired their BARS and Garands into their faces. During a fight in one of the gun-pits, an enemy shell had exploded, and every man in the pit—Jap and Marine—was killed.

That night, as our tired survivors dug into their holes several hundred yards ahead of the ridge, it seemed as if progress had been made. Many of the Jap positions in the high ground had fallen. We were pushing, painfully but surely, through the heart of the enemy's Iwo defenses. All we had to do was keep going. Eventually we would reach the sea—only a couple of miles to the north.

But the Japs had other ideas.

In the middle of the night they came back underground. When our men pushed out the next morning, they didn't know that the enemy was behind them. But the rear elements, coming up in reserve, discovered to their dismay that, even though the big Jap guns and mortars were being eliminated, there was no safety on Iwo so long as one uncaptured enemy remained alive. Beginning that morning, the Japs in that ridge waged a struggle against our rear that was typical of fights in many supposedly secured areas.

Early in the morning Dr. Jost's aid station, still following the troops, had set up in a small amphitheater formed by the rocks at one end of the ridge. Our men were again in action up ahead, and the stretcher-bearers were bringing back a stream of wounded. A heavy Jap machine gun suddenly rattled from the side of the ridge. A man carrying a crate of ammunition had been passing by. He dropped his load of mortar shells, looked startled, and crumpled in a heap in the sand. A group of riflemen, idling across the open space, hit the dirt and wriggled behind rocks. They tried to see where the bullets were coming from, for the ridge had supposedly been freed of Japs. The men spotted an opening in the rocks and fired at it. The Jap machine gun ceased rattling. The Marines clambered out of the shellholes and crawled toward the ridge. Other men, sensing a fight, waved to each other and began to close in. Covering each other with carbines and rifles, they edged slowly toward the rocky hole.

A blaze of Jap small-arms fire came from different parts of the ridge. The bullets whistled past the men in the aid station. A corpsman looked up, bewildered, and came around the ridge to see what all the shooting was about.

"Get down!" a Marine yelled at him.

The corpsman dropped behind a rock and pushed his helmet back on his head. "Hey," he called. "Knock it off. This here's a hospital."

The men didn't appreciate the humor. They pointed down the road behind him. The corpsman turned. Four stretcher-bearers were stumbling along the road with a wounded man, hurrying to the aid station.

The corpsman cupped his hands over his mouth to try to warn the stretcher-bearers, but there was too much noise and they couldn't hear him. The Japs began to fire at them. They ran faster. Then a bullet hit one of them in the leg. He looked around wildly and crashed to the ground. The stretcher spilled on top of him. The men in front tripped as they tried to hold on to the stretcher. The Japs kept shooting into the group. The wounded stretcher-bearer jumped up again and grabbed his end of the litter. He started to drag the stretcher along, but dropped it. The man on the stretcher hung half over it, his head and shoulders dragging along the ground.

The other men half-crawled and half-ran with the stretcher until they reached the rocks. The wounded stretcher-bearer loped after them. When he reached the shelter, he fell again. It was a miracle that he had been able to stay on his feet, for the bullet had laid open his calf as if it had been hit by a meat cleaver. The man on the stretcher was stone-dead; one of the bullets from the ridge had hit him in the skull.

No one knew how many Japs were in the ridge. A supply captain, coming up from the rear, saw what was going on and radioed for tanks and demolitions men. More Marines from neighboring units gathered. They inspected the ridge from safety points behind rocks.

When the tanks arrived, the men started the step-by-step job of again cleaning out the ridge. They threw smoke bombs against the rocks and moved in with bazookas and automatic weapons. When the smoke drifted away they had to shoot fast, or a Jap would catch them from one of the many holes. The tanks hurled their 75s at every position the gunners could locate. Engineers tried to fling dynamite charges into the caves. Despite their preponderance of weapons, the Marines found that there were too many holes. They would attack one, only to be shot at from another one half a dozen feet away.

Finally flame-throwers were called. They threw long jets of flaming liquid into the holes and along the curving walls of the tunnels. The roaring flames did the trick. The Marines heard the Japs howling. A few rushed out of the caves on fire. The men shot them or knocked them down and beat out the flames and took them prisoners. When the Marines began to hear muffled explosions inside the caves, they guessed that some of the Japs were blowing themselves up with hand grenades.

Soon the flame-throwers paused. A Marine lifted himself cautiously into view. There were no shots from the caves. A Jap with his clothes in rags hunched himself out of one hole, his arms upraised. The Marines stood up behind the rocks and waved to him to come out. The Jap indicated that there were more who would like to surrender. The Marines motioned him to tell them to come out.

Almost forty scared and beaten men emerged from various holes. Some of them had round pudding faces. They grinned nervously and said they were Koreans who had been forced by the Japs to stay in the caves. They said that everyone else in the caves had either been burned to death or committed suicide.

Our men sent them to the rear. Gruggen drove some of them back in his jeep ambulance. A few of the wounded and badly burned enemy were treated at our aid station. Our men stood around sullenly while the doctors administered plasma to them—something the enemy would never have done for us.

At the ridge the Marines groped cautiously among the rocks from hole to hole, examining each entrance-way. Dead bodies, some hit by bullets and grenade fragments, some burned into frightful black lumps, lay in the holes. The smell was overwhelming, and the men turned away in disgust.

The battle of the ridge seemed over. An officer made a note to bring up demolition crews as soon as they could be spared by the front-line companies. They would seal up the holes in this troublesome ridge. The Marines gathered their casualties and drifted away. The tanks shifted into reverse and backed out. Peacefulness settled once more over the area.

But it was not for long.

Soon afterwards, Reid Chamberlain paused at the aid station. He was running a message up to Able Company, dug in among the rocks several hundred yards ahead, and he asked me to accompany him.

We began to cross the clearing which we thought had been rid of Jap sniper fire. To escape occasional mortar shells that were dropping in the open, we clung closely to the rocky walls of the ridge, intending to follow the longer semicircular, but safer, route to the company. Gruggen, whose ambulance was parked at the aid station waiting for casualties, went with us. He wanted to see the caves from which the Japs had just been burned.

We were picking our way among the stones and the burned Jap bodies when three shots rang out from the hillside. We tried to run behind some boulders. Chamberlain drew his pistol and looked hastily around. There was another shot. We heard a thud. We thought the bullet had struck the curving side of the ridge.

When we reached safe spots, we paused and looked back. Chamberlain was nowhere in sight. Gruggen and an automatic rifleman, who had been coming the other way, were crouched behind near-by rocks, their teeth clenched, their hands gripping their weapons. They were trying to find the hole from which the shots had come. We called Chamberlain but received no answer. Slowly we tried to edge back. Rifle shots cracked at us from several holes, and we ducked again.

The long, rocky ridge was once more alive with enemy. Again Marines began to gather, coming up cautiously to help us. They dashed from rock to rock and slid among the boulders, trying to seek cover from the many caves that looked out at us. We told them about Chamberlain, lying somewhere among the rocks. We formed a fire team and began crawling forward. When the Japs fired at us again, the men covering us saw where the shots were coming from. They sent a stream of automatic fire at the holes and "buttoned up" the Japs. One burly sergeant stood straight up without a helmet on and, gritting his teeth, fired his carbine from his hip, moving directly at a hole as he fired. One of the men finally reached Chamberlain's body and lifted his head. A trickle of blood flowed from behind his ear. His eyes were open, but he was dead.

There was nothing we could say or do. We felt stunned, angry, frustrated. We could have fired point-blank the rest of the day at those holes. The Japs would only have laughed at us. In an instant they had claimed one of our best men. Chamberlain's wonderful war record had ended abruptly. After so many heroic deeds, it seemed an added tragedy that he was killed while doing nothing but walking.

We crawled back and sent for flame-throwers, only to find we couldn't get any more that day; they were all busy up front. Meanwhile an outfit of the 9th Marines was moving up and pitching its bivouac on top of the ridge, which had become silent again. We hunted up the commanding officer and told him there were still Japs inside the hill. We related to him all that had happened at the ridge that day. He listened concernedly but decided it was too late in the afternoon to try to root out the Japs still in the caves. He posted guards behind the rocks facing the ridge and gave them orders to keep all straggling Marines away from the holes.

That night tragedy struck again. After dark some of the Japs tried to come out of their holes. The Marine guards saw them moving among the rocks and opened fire, killing some and driving others back in. The Japs screamed and howled when they realized they were trapped, and began to commit suicide.

On top of the ridge the Marines who were dug in could hear grenades exploding in the underground caverns beneath them, as the Japs killed themselves. Suddenly, towards midnight, there was a terrific blast that rocked the whole hill. Huge boulders flew among the Marines. Some of the men were hurled into the air. Others were buried in their foxholes as hot sand poured in on them.

A flash of flame shot into the sky and there was a series of rumbles and more explosions. Rocks, dirt, and hunks of concrete showered among the startled Marines. By the light of the flames, the men dug each other out and scrambled down the ridge to safety. Stones cascaded after them in landslides that sealed up half the holes in the ridge's wall. The men took up positions behind the rocks and waited for the Japs to come out. A platoon sergeant saw two of the enemy sitting dazedly among the stones; they were carrying antipersonnel mines around their waists. He killed them as they tried to get up. Another man struggling down the slope saw other Japs trying to rush out from the holes, only to be buried in landslides; their arms and legs protruded from the dirt and rocks.

Slowly our men realized what had happened: The Japs had blown themselves up and, with them, the whole ridge. When dawn came, the Marines discovered that they had suffered only one serious casualty. Many men had been completely buried by the rocks and sulphur ashes, but companions had dug them out before they had smothered. Scouts who poked into some of the remaining holes found that the Japs had used land mines and 125-pound aerial bombs to blow up the hill.

That day our demolitions men began the tedious job of trying to seal all the cave entrances in the ridge. It soon became evident that sealing all the openings was out of the question. The men worked all day, placing charges in the mouths of more than forty caves. When they were blown, we couldn't tell but that cracks had been left through which Japs could still fire. By evening everyone felt a sense of frustration and anticipated further trouble, since there were still many caves unsealed. The demolitions men gave it up; they were needed more urgently elsewhere. Someone said: "We ought to put up a sign here; 'Pass at your own risk.'" Then they left.

A day or two later a supply unit moved into the area. The unit pitched tents and galleys, built ration piles, parked jeeps and trailers, and nonchalantly went about its business of shuttling hot food, ammunition, and water to the battalions ahead.

In the afternoon a jeep and trailer set off for the front lines with hot coffee and doughnuts. It passed the ridge and was fired on. The driver didn't wait to find out what kind of weapon was shooting at him—he knew it was something big, so he stepped on the gas and raced out of the area. On the way back he was shot at again. Jeep ambulance drivers and other supply men reported similar attacks on them. Finally a tank, lumbering over the road, was hit. The crew jumped out and hid behind some rocks.

After a while they came back and reported that an anti-tank gun was somewhere among the debris of the ridge. Another tank was sent up. It waited behind some rocks till the Jap gun fired and showed its position. Then the tank blasted at it with its 75. In a few moments the Jap position was a pile of smoking rubble. Automatic riflemen who moved in to catch enemy survivors found the weapon to be a 47 mm. antitank gun. The Japs had kept it concealed during all the previous fighting around the ridge.

It would seem that this should have ended the story of the ridge, but it didn't. As the battle for Iwo progressed, Jap riflemen and machine gunners continued to hang on inside the tunnels and fire out at passersby whenever good shots were presented. A wireman, stringing a telephone line between rear command posts, was shot through the head. Two cooks were winged in the arms. A whole mortar platoon was pinned down in its holes by a Jap gunner. A barber and an officer who was having his hair cut were sent running by a burst of rifle shots.

Whenever our men could spot exact positions from which Japs were firing, they tried to knock them out. With auto-matic rifles and bazookas, they crept among the rocks and blasted at the small holes. Then they threw dynamite charges into the slits and hoped those would do the trick.

It was an almost hopeless task. On D plus 25, the day we overran the last bit of Iwo Jima to secure the island, death was still coming from the ridge. A Jap sniper that day shot a passing corpsman through the ear.

XI

"I'm Saying Goodbye to You All"

Wₕᵢₗₑ our 1st battalion was making progress through its section of the Jap-held high ground, our entire line across the island was advancing slowly but steadily. On our extreme right the 4th Marine Division seized the highest point on Iwo except Suribachi—Hill 382—and opened the way for the securing of its zone of action. On the left side of the line the 5th Marine Division slugged its way painfully up the western coast of the island, losing many men among the wild ridges and gulleys. And in the center the 3d Division—the 9th Marines and the other battalions of the 21st—paced the general advance in a move that was knifing through the Jap positions and threatening to cut the enemy in two.

On the day we first seized the ridge where Chamberlain was killed, the 3d battalion of the 21st, on our right flank, moved ahead of the northern end of the second airfield and captured the town of Motoyama, the largest settlement on the island. Before the war about eleven hundred people had lived there, working in the sulphur mine and in a sugar refinery near by. But prior to our landing on Iwo all the civilians had been evacuated.

Again Gruggen's ambulance had been the first vehicle through the narrow, twisting sand road that led past Moto-

189

yama. Jap stragglers were still in the area, and they fired at him from concealed positions.

"What kind of a town is it?" we asked Gruggen when he told us of the 3d battalion's progress.

"They didn't build buildings there," he answered angrily. "They built pillboxes. It's nothing but a bunch of rocks and forts."

The 3d battalion followed its capture of Motoyama by pushing across the third airfield on the island. It was a rough clearing in the sulphur-mine area. The Japs had never completed the runways, but they had had to press the field into use after our pre-invasion bombing attacks had chewed up the other two airfields. About twenty wrecked Jap planes stood in the clearing. The area around the field was a wilderness of tumbled rocks, slag heaps, smoking sulphur mounds, and tall, jagged ridges—a paradise for snipers. For many days the open airfield was a death trap for our men who tried to run across it.

The ground in this northern part of the island steamed from the sulphur deposits, and the sand burned us when we tried to dig foxholes. Some of our men cooked their C rations by setting cans in the loose yellow-and-white earth. At night we had to lie on blankets and ponchos to keep from being burned. One man died when the wall of his hole fell in on him while he was sleeping. We found him in the morning partly buried in the hot sand.

As we drove the Japs out of their artillery and mortar positions in the high ground, we thought that our rate of casualties would drop sharply. But it didn't. The fighting became more intense and close-in among the chasms and rocky ridges, and the Japs relied more on their small arms and knee mortars. They waited for us in their holes and made us expose ourselves trying to find them. Then when we were in the open and almost upon them, they picked us off from the front, the rear, and both sides. However, with the elimination of most of the Jap heavy weapons, our rear was freed from harassing fire, and reinforcements and supplies poured onto Iwo's beaches to help us push our attack to conclusion.

Each day an unbroken stream of replacements trudged up to the front to fill the big holes in our units. Some of them were veterans of earlier fights against the Japs—Guadalcanal, Tarawa, and Cape Gloucester. Some of them were boots, going into their first combat. They had come over together from the States and had been landed early in the Iwo operation to help unload supplies on the beaches. Now, as they were needed, they were sent to the front. We watched them pick their way carefully among the rocks and past the sulphur mounds to report to commanding officers and be assigned to the various units. They were joined by other "replacements"—volunteers from our headquarters and rear elements: communications men, clerks, drivers, service personnel, and others who knew how great was the demand at the front for additional riflemen and machine gunners. As at Guam, the insistence that every Marine be trained as a combat man again paid off.

Among those in our rear units who asked to be allowed to fill in at the front were twenty-one members of the 3d Division's war-dog platoon. The men left their dogs back at the first airfield and went up to the front lines as riflemen.

Platoon Sergeant Alfred N. Edwards, who led the detail of dog-handlers-turned-infantry men, told us later what happened to them.

"We started forward time after time," he said, "only to get stopped after about fifty yards by machine-gun bullets. The Japs hid behind every rock and stone and filled the air with bullets. And if they didn't hit you head-on, bullets ricocheted back at you off the rocks. A lot of us never even saw the Japs. It was hard knowing just where they were. One of our men got shot through the mouth. We thought we saw where the bullets came from. We looked over there—and another guy got shot from the opposite direction."

In a few days Edwards's unit lost four men killed and seven wounded.

Men who weren't hit among the rocks counted themselves lucky. There were a thousand near-misses a day; to many a man a fraction of an inch meant life. A Jap grenade landed at the feet of Corporal John B. Fennell and exploded; the fragments whizzed harmlessly around him. Sergeant L. D. Southwell had his helmet pierced during a firefight; he didn't know it until he combed his hair and felt a slight welt on the top of his head—then he looked at his helmet and almost passed out. A rifleman with the 21st, Private Robert W. Swayne, had a bullet sideswipe his helmet with such force that the steel was curled back; about all it did was give Swayne a good headache.

Meanwhile, in the center of our cross-island line, the 2nd battalion of the 21st went into action again and strove to break through the last Jap defenses and reach the northern shore. The 2nd battalion was led by its executive officer, Major George A. Percy, a former stockbroker who had joined the paymaster section of the Marine Corps when he was forty-five years old, had then argued himself into a combat command, was wounded twice in one day by mortar fragments, but refused to leave his men. At night he had a stretcher brought up to sleep on, because his wounds made sleeping on the rocks too painful. Day after day he led his men personally across the rocky mounds, hurrying them on in an attempt to be the first unit to break through to the sea. On D plus 15 one of his lieutenants, commanding G Company, finally led two platoons to the top of a ridge and, four hundred yards away, sighted the water on Iwo's northern shore.

It was an exciting moment, but only a moment. The Japs were entrenched in force on both flanks, and the Marines were only a handful. Two men went back for help. Only one got through; the other was wounded. Eight demolition men and flame-throwers were dispatched from the rear, but none of them reached the platoons on the ridge. Stretcher-bearers found two of them a few hours later; the other six were missing in action. The position was too hot for G Company to hold. The men had to withdraw. The next day, however, Major Percy led the whole battalion up to the ridge and this time held. But the men could not go down to the water; the flanks were not secured. So the 2nd battalion lost the race.

The first outfit to reach the water went down the cliffs to the beach the next day, D plus 17. It was our old friend, Able Company of the 1st battalion—at least, what was left of Able Company. Out of more than two hundred men who had landed on Iwo with that outfit two and a half weeks before, only three were left; all the rest of the men fighting under the command of Able Company were replacements.

Twenty-eight of the Company's new men slid down a three-hundred-yard rocky slope, studded with pillboxes and cave positions, all of which had been silenced by naval gun-fire earlier in the campaign. The men stood on the beach, awed by the fact that they had sliced the Jap positions in two. Some of the men took off their shoes and socks and bathed their feet in the refreshing sea water. Suddenly a Jap mortar shell crashed on the beach fifty yards away. The men scrambled back to the rocks. Another shell crashed, and fragments hit seven men. Three fell with serious wounds. The men formed litter teams and carried the casualties halfway back up the cliff to a ledge where a command post had been established. Later, men again went down to the sand and filled a canteen with sea water. They sent it back through channels to General Erskine with a note: "Forwarded for approval, not for consumption."

As our other units ground forward through the rocky gulleys to come out on the cliffs facing the sea, more and more of the old men who had come through Bougainville and Guam disappeared from the ranks. Luck ran out here and there, and our companions of past days fell by the wayside. Every time the jeep ambulances went by, the drivers called out to us the names of the wounded men inside, because they knew that we would recognize them. One day Walter Page was taken out; he had been hit by a Jap hand grenade. The same day a

Major whose family I had known in the United States was evacuated by Gruggen. One of the Major's legs had been amputated at a front-line aid station. He was wrapped in blankets. His face was yellow, his eyes closed, his mouth wide open. A corpsman rode to the beach with him, giving him whole blood all the way. At the beach a doctor at the evacuation station thought the Major was dying, but he reached a hospital ship and was saved.

Near the end of the campaign Joe Young, the scout who had been allowed to keep the '03 bolt-action rifle, who had found the headless Chamorros on Guam, and who had been the only man in our outfit who never received mail, was hit squarely by a Jap shell. We never even found the remnants of the shiny old rifle he had loved so dearly. On another day a Marine we all knew and liked was reported missing. We found him two days later lying on his stomach near a mound of sulphur. He had no legs, and his torn buttocks were a mass of ugly green flesh.

Those last days on Iwo reminded us of our first days on the beachhead at Guam when it had seemed as if we were losing men every minute. Death and injury again were commonplace. It was good news if we heard that a man had been only slightly wounded. We talked once more of "million-dollar wounds." Stretcher-bearers one morning carried back a man with a mangled leg—a burly flame-thrower from Tennessee, who still had enough strength to support himself on his elbows on the stretcher. He half sat up, grinning at everyone he passed and shouting: "So long, everybody! I'm going back to the States. I been wounded. I'm saying goodbye to you all. I been wounded!" The men laughed and felt strangely happy for him as they watched him go by. He had done a good job. And he had fared better than most of the other flame-throwers. They had been killed—or taken out so badly hurt that no one could have laughed.

Soon after our units pulled up even along the northern coast, some of our men turned back to mop up the sulphur

area and the region around the third airfield. Hundreds of
Japs were still holed up in the rocks and ridges, and bullets
flew wildly in all directions. At the same time other men
returned to the vicinity of Motoyama to rest, before helping
the 5th Division secure its zone of action on the western side
of the island. Among the units granted respite was Easy (E)
Company of the 21st. The men bivouacked among the rocks
near the sulphur mine and had their first hot chow in ten
days. Easy Company was part of the 2d battalion. I had not
been with it, and I went over to see how the men had come
through the campaign. Most of my friends were gone, though
it appeared that the company had had the best luck in the
regiment as far as casualties were concerned: they had thirty
survivors of the original roster of more than two hundred
men, the largest number of survivors in any company in the
regiment.

Among these was a nineteen-year-old Pfc named Horace
Brown from Washington, D.C. He and I had joined the
Marine Corps on the same day two years before, and had
gone through boot camp at Parris Island, S.C., together.
After that, our paths had separated until Brown had appeared
on Guam one day as a replacement for the 21st Marines. He
took my hand excitedly when he saw me on Iwo, and grinned
through a stubble of beard. His face and teeth were black
from his many days of hugging the island's sand.

"Gosh," he exclaimed, "I never expected to be alive this
long!"

Brown had had many narrow escapes, like most of the rest
of us. Once he had been caught in the open on the second
airfield and had lain in the sand behind a six-inch mound while
his buddies were picked off, one by one, by the Japs. Finally
the Marines dropped a mortar barrage in front of him, and
he was able to escape. Another time he had crawled seventy-
five yards across the open under enemy machine-gun fire to
bring back a lieutenant who had been wounded.

We sat awhile among the rocks, not saying much. We had

to keep low to duck bullets that were flying in all directions from mopping-up firefights taking place among the jagged ridges. Squads of the 9th and 21st Marines were trying to root out Japs who were still dug in around us, and the Japs were replying to our men's fire.

"Well," I said finally to Brown, "it will be nice when the war's over. When we get back to Washington, we'll have a steak dinner together."

"Check," he said, and added, "if we ever do get back to Washington."

An orderly came running up with a handful of mail. He knelt down behind a boulder, sorted the letters, and called the men's names. Some of the men dashed across the open to get their letters. Others wearily asked Marines nearer the orderly to pass the mail to them. Every time the orderly called the name of someone who had been killed or wounded, the men would look at each other, and a sergeant would yell out; "KIA" or "WIA"—killed in action or wounded in action.

Brown looked at me thoughtfully. I prepared to go. A corporal beside us, who had waited expectantly for a letter and didn't get any, dug his fist into the smelly sulphuric sand and twisted his hand around in the hole as if he were in pain. There were tears in his eyes.

I said goodbye to Brown and returned to Division head-quarters. The next day Easy Company went back in the lines to help the 5th Division secure its zone of action. Brown lived through the rest of the campaign, but some of the other men in Easy Company didn't. The corporal who had dug his fist into the sand was killed on D plus 25—the day Iwo Jima was called secured.

Before the end of the campaign, we took a few more prisoners. We had a Division stockade near the first airfield. Some of our prisoners were Koreans, who seemed happy to be free of the Japs and anxious to help us. As soon as we had established their identity, our men treated them sympathet-ically. The Japanese prisoners behaved like the ones we had taken on Guam. They were afraid at first that we were going to kill them. Every time we approached them, they bowed and hissed through their teeth. Then, when we gave them food and medical attention, they brooded over whether they had committed an error in allowing themselves to be taken alive. They had disgraced themselves and indicated that their Emperor would be displeased.

It irritated our MPs. "Everything's the Emperor!" one of them exclaimed. "They do anything he says. If he had told them it was okay to surrender, this lousy battle would have been over a long time ago."

Some of us felt like adding that, if the Emperor had been against his militarists and their policies in the first place, there might never have been this lousy Pacific war.

On the day the 5th Division's sector was finally overrun and the last square yard of Iwo's surface was in our hands, I received sudden orders recalling me for special duty in the United States. I tried to visit the different units in our regiment to say goodbye to friends who were still on the island. I was unable, however, to reach many of the outfits. They were still pinned down among the rocks by Jap small-arms fire. It seemed that, even though we had every square yard of Iwo's surface, the Japs still held thousands of square yards below the surface. It was to take many days and more casualties before the mopping-up of Iwo's thousands of caves and tunnels and underground caverns would be complete. Ten days after the island was called secured, two hundred Japs emerged just before dawn from holes in the ground, charged into an Army Air Corps encampment, and killed pilots and ground crewmen in their tents. Finally all the enemy were wiped out by members of a near-by Marine engineer outfit. But new units, who were still arriving on the island, came to know (as we had learned on Guam) that there was danger so long as there was one Jap alive, still willing to die for the Emperor.

The first airfield, from which I left, was swarming with

planes. While we had been fighting in the center of the island, Seabees and aviation engineers had repaired the field. They had worked under fire, and some men had been killed and wounded by harassing Jap mortar and artillery shells. But during the second week of battle a crippled B-29 had landed on the field, and once again we had seen tangible fruits of our men's sacrifices. The Superfort had been damaged in a raid over Tokyo; if it hadn't been for the field on Iwo, the plane would have fallen into the sea, trying to get back to the Marianas seven hundred and fifty miles away. Later it was announced that during the first hundred days after Iwo was secured, 851 B-29s—more than nine thousand flyers—had found safety on Iwo. We lost approximately four thousand five hundred Marines fighting for the island, but in one hundred days twice that number of men had been saved.

I flew to Guam in an Army plane, then changed to a Navy transport plane, and went on to Kwajalein, Johnston Island, and Pearl Harbor. It was like taking a regular flight in the United States. Passenger and cargo planes made the run every day, maintaining schedules between stops thousands of miles apart, and thinking nothing of it. When I had sailed overseas the year before, it had taken me twenty-four days to cross the Pacific from San Francisco to New Caledonia. We had had to steam on a great circle southward to avoid Jap-held islands. Now we flew over those same islands, and most of them were in our hands.

Four days after leaving the sand and bullets of Iwo Jima— seven hundred miles from Tokyo—I was home. The United States looked wonderful. The first night I went into a restaurant and asked for a steak.

"For goodness' sakes!" the waitress exclaimed. "Where have you been?"

The process of going from one world to another had begun.

Appendix

TRANSCRIPT of the eyewitness description of the landing on Guam, July 21, 1944, made for radio broadcast in the United States. The recording began in the hold of the transport at 0600, D-day morning:

"American transports are lying all around us. In a few minutes Marines will begin streaming down the sides of these ships into tiny landing boats. It is not yet H-hour. We are still far out from land. But we are getting into the small boats early in case of Japanese air attacks. It is better to have all troops and supplies off the bigger ships, which are the first targets for enemy planes.

"Right now we're in the very noisy hold of our transport—our living quarters. They are hoisting landing boats away from the top of the hold so that the light is coming in on us. Marines are huddling around waiting for the call to man the debarkation nets and go over the side. We are with a tank destroyer unit. We are speaking from a halftrack as we wait for it to be raised from this hold and lowered over the side of this ship and into a tank lighter. This halftrack, like the Marine tanks, is attached to the assault infantry. It will move in early as direct support for the infantry. We will go along with it. We will be in the first trip of boats from this ship. So any minute we expect to hear the order to hoist away and raise us out of this hold.

"We're all equipped and ready for storming the beach. We've taken over a good part of the inside of this halftrack with our equipment. There's a lot of ammunition here for both the 75 mm. cannon and the two machine guns which are mounted on both sides. There are also boxes of hand grenades and the packs and equipment of some of the men who are going ashore with us.

"And now I'd like to ask one of the Marines down here how he feels on this morning of combat just before it's time to go over the side. He comes from Southern California. [Security regulations prohibited my mentioning his name.] What's your job going to be?"

"Take 50-caliber machine guns up in support of our 2d battalion."

"How do you feel this morning?"

"A little bit nervous."

"You think everybody feels that way?"

"I don't know if they all feel the same way I do. I feel like a ten-year-old kid who put a nickle in a one-arm rounder and won all the money and didn't know what to do with it."

"You've been in combat before?"

"Yes. Bougainville."

"Did you come through it all right that time?"

"I got a Purple Heart."

"Well, I hope you don't get one this time. Are you thinking about back home at all this morning?"

"Oh, yeah. Wish I were back there. Got a wife and child."

"Well, thanks a lot and good luck to you. And now we've gotten orders to be raised out of the hold and we're being lifted up by braces. As we leave the hold we can see the Marines who are still waiting for orders to man their own debarkation nets and go down into their own boats sitting around and lying around the sides of the hold on their bunks. They are quiet. They stare at each other. They don't say anything. They watch each other's actions very closely as though their own lives depended on it. Several men are in-

THE JAPS ASKED FOR IT. Flamethrowers at work on Iwo.

WHERE CHAMBERLAIN WAS KILLED. While riflemen cover holes in the ridge, a flame-thrower goes to work on the cave from which Chamberlain was shot.

tently watching one man who's just calmly and deliberately tightening the laces on his leggings. And here we go up out of the hold. We're rising above the forward part of the ship. We're being swung over by the giant boom. The winches are creaking and the donkey engine roaring. We can see Marines standing all around us now on the decks in their green dungarees—some of them in camouflaged dungarees. And they've got on their steel helmets, their weapons and packs on their backs. They're all ready to go over when their individual debarkation net calls ring out. We had two good omens yesterday. We saw an eclipse of the sun yesterday afternoon. We hope that it means the eclipse of the Rising Sun. That eclipse was not visible in most of the world, just in this particular part. Then last night we had the good news that Premier Tojo has resigned in Japan. We don't know who's going to follow him, but, whoever it is, we'll try to help take care of him too.

"And now we're going down the side of the ship toward the water. A tank lighter is under us. You can probably hear its motor. There are Marines already in the tank lighter. They're ordering us down. We just hit the side of the tank lighter. We're coming down in. We can see the water and ships all around us—everything: transports, warships, LSTs. We're bouncing around here. They haven't put us down steadily yet. They're still trying to steer us into the well of the tank lighter. It's a pretty big ship but kind of narrow for a half-track. The sailors above us are hollering down. They are Seabees who are specially with us to load and unload this ship. There are many planes in the sky—American planes. We haven't seen any Jap resistance yet. Here we are bouncing down now into the tank lighter. Marines are grabbing hold of the sides of this halftrack trying to pull us in.

"We got up early this morning and we went up on deck and we saw a show! It was pitch black but we saw all kinds of lights on the horizon. They were American warships shelling Guam. There were star clusters and great flashes and explosions of white, yellow, and red lights; and, as it grew light, we began to see the outlines of ships around us and saw our own convoy steaming in. We could imagine what the Japs must have thought when, as dawn broke, they saw our convoy moving in behind the protective screen of our ships that had been shelling them. I've got to duck now as they loosen the braces that took us up out of the hold and over the side into the tank lighter, because one of them is liable to swing and hit me in the head, and even though I've got my steel helmet on it makes quite a crack. I'm lying stretched on my back—an ungraceful position. We can see many faces of men looking over the side of the transport down on us, giving orders, yelling at each other, and I think they'll free us very soon. One brace is caught over the 75mm. gun that protrudes past the driver's seat.

"All right. We're free now. —You can get hurt in the funniest ways! —And now our tank lighter's motor has started up again, and the cargo net has dropped to us, and here come the Marines down! The few Marines who were in our tank lighter had come down specially to bring down this halftrack. Now here come the combat members of our team hand over hand, reaching with their feet for the rungs of the cargo net. And if you've ever done it, you know it's quite a trick to come down these things, especially with packs on your backs. They're red-faced, but, boy, they know how to come down in regular rhythm. The gun commander of this halftrack is keeping them away from coming into the halftrack so that they come into the tank lighter instead. They've got leggings on because they have to wade across the reef later. Their helmets either have camouflaged covers or are spotted with green and brown paint. They have a combat pack, and that's just the top half of the pack. It's usually just full of socks, rations, and maybe a shirt and some soap—and a bayonet sticking along the side of it. Various weapons on their backs, ranging from M1 rifles to carbines—automatics, knives, sawed-off bayonets at their sides. They have two canteens apiece because we might be without water for quite a while until they're sure that the water on Guam is good enough to drink. Some of them have entrenching tools—shovels, and others picks—because we don't know just what the terrain will be like where we have to dig in. They've all got gas masks and some have dust protectors to put over their mouths and noses. And they're still coming down. They have ponchos too, rolled up around their blankets—some without any blankets at all—just ponchos or a shelter half, camouflaged, as you may know, on one side in various shades of splotched brown, on the other side various colors of splotched green. Here comes a fellow with a tremendous knife. Here's a fellow with a cigar box hanging on his side. Another one with a magazine. Some of them with rope hanging down, and gloves so they can move easily through the sword grass that we expect will be here. They're coming straight down, hand over hand, from above. Here comes one with binoculars and a pistol. Their big, heavy shoes are going to come in very handy when they cross the reef. They're going to have to keep the water out. They're going to have to stay in those shoes the rest of the day and for many days. So we hope our shoes don't get too wet.

"And now, looking around, there are some boats already filled with men—Marines from some of the other transports. A few from this transport have already gotten away. They are the LCVPs—the little Higgins boats, built down around New Orleans and in many parts of the United States, and they are rendezvousing near us already, going around in circles as they come up for different waves.

"We are leaving the side of the transport now. We're fully packed. All our men are in. Some of them are yelling at each other. They seem to have lost their nervousness. There's a friend waving down at us good luck—'Get some Japs for me!' He's a sailor up there on gun watch. We leave the prow of the transport that brought us, and we feel we're leaving a good friend. We don't know what's ahead, but we know it won't be as comfortable as it was on that transport. We can see the boys up on the transport waving down at us, and now we're moving away to join our particular wave.

"H-hour has not yet come, and we're not going in immediately. The shelling is still continuing, and we who are going to land as soon as the shelling from the warships stops will stay out in these little boats, going around and around in circles according to the various waves to which we belong. There are many of these individual circles out here. What happens is that the men get off the ship according to the wave that they're in. We're in what is known as the second wave of the first trip of boats. That means the first wave goes a couple of minutes ahead of us, and we come right afterwards. There are quite a few of these little landing boats in each wave. However, we are the only tank lighter—or, as we're called, an LCM—in this wave. There may be another one coming from another ship. The other halftrack that was in our hold goes to another wave altogether. It comes in about two waves behind us.

"Now, again looking around, there are many ships in this area, standing just off the beachhead at Guam. The transports are now all around us. We're moving away from them, leaving them behind. We're just passing now one of the control boats, a boat much larger than this one but still not a very big one, fully equipped with radio and signaling devices to order the waves forward from this particular point up to the next control point. Some of the landing boats are now pulling up to the sides of the transports to get the waves that are coming after us. They've been empty all this time, and we can see them pulling up to get more men.

"We're going forward now—not actually into the beach yet, but we're moving up to find our own circle and go around with it in a safe, convenient spot. We're out of range—we're miles out from Guam. That may sound strange, but out here the transports stay out a pretty good distance, and the little boats take the men in to the various control points. It's still too far away to see the beach, and from way out here the island looks something like a smudge rising pretty high on both sides. Between us and the island at the moment are many ships, most of them warships and LSTs with assault troops and amphibious tractors that will take the men across the reef.

"A control boat has just come up to us and is asking our number. They want to know where we're going. We have radiomen aboard, and they can stay in touch with the various groups and boats that are controlling our waves and the groups that we're supposed to go in with. Incidentally, we're towing a little rubber boat behind this tank lighter, and inside the tank lighter we have a trailer which our halftrack will pull. It's full of flame-throwers which will be used by some of our men.

"We're turning now and beginning to move in again, looking for our rendezvous area. Now we can see Guam very well, though it's still very far away. We're surprised at how big it is. It's very much like Guadalcanal. It looks kind of purplish and brown from here now, and still somewhat misty. Straight ahead of us is the beach we will land on. It's a concave beach about two thousand yards long, lying between two high, wooded points that jut out. On the left is Adelup Point. It has a large, spread-out house like a hacienda on its summit. In peacetime it was a fine residence with many rooms. Now it probably hides some small Jap arms, because I don't think there's very much left of that house after our Naval shelling. There certainly can't be any big stuff left there. On the right is Asan Point, and a little way out from it in the water is a rock called Camel Rock. When H-hour strikes—which will be soon—we will land between those points.

"The beach is only about six yards deep. Then there are some coconut trees with dense undergrowth, and a road that runs parallel to the beach. On the other side of the road are some native houses. In one part ahead of us they're clustered together, and that is the village of Asan. To the right is the village of Nagas, and way over to our left, not directly in the line of our attack on this beach, is the capital city of Agana.

Behind the road that runs along the beach the terrain rises abruptly. There are cliffs that some of us must scale or go around. They are called the Chonito Cliffs. We expect trouble getting up them. Then there are steep, grassy hills and valleys covered with sword grass from ankle to chest-high. That grass cuts you badly when you push through it, they say. But we understand that our planes are going to try to burn it down ahead of us with incendiaries. Far to our right, out of the immediate range of action, are the Piti Navy Yard and Apra Harbor, together with Cabras Island. These are objectives which we'll go after, once our beachhead is secured. That is the scene from our present position off the beach.

"Now we estimate that there are about 30,000 Japs on Guam, veterans of fighting in China and Manchuria. There are about 23,000 civilians, most of whom we think will be friendly to us. It's still not H-hour yet. The sun is getting very bright and a little hot now. The sky is blue—there are puffy, white clouds in it all around us on the horizon. It hasn't rained, thank goodness, although it looked like it earlier in the morning, and it still may. And out here Marines are still streaming out of holds on the various transports and climbing over the sides in units, coming down the swaying cargo nets like brown waterfalls, hand over hand, into the landing boats.

"There's quite a bit of naval firing going on around us. Earlier this morning we saw battleships, destroyers, cruisers —everything—firing. Very near us now is an LSD—one of the big, new Landing Ships, Dock, which take care of small boats. It's a unique-looking ship, with high bulkheads coming way up in the forward part to hold the ships it takes in to repair. Looking out over the LCM, I see an LCI going past us now. I'm standing up a minute to look around. We're still out of range—I hope.

"Now there's the whole beachhead ahead of us, smoking from one end to the other! You can't see anything through that smoke now. There have probably been an awful lot of hits registered this morning. This place has been fired on by our Navy and Air Force for sixteen days now. However, we've not raised our hopes too high; we'd rather be pleasantly surprised, because we want to be shown that naval gunfire can knock out all those emplacements that we know are there. We think they have probably done a wonderful job, especially on the very big stuff, but we're skeptical about the mortar fire that's going to come at us from very well entrenched places, particularly back from the beach about 1,000 to 5,000 yards up in the ridges where the naval gunfire can't get at them very well.

"Now we are going in in the first wave that will walk across the reef. The assault infantry will be carried over the reef in amphibious tractors. The tractors will take them right up onto the beach and into the face of the enemy. Because we cannot transfer our halftrack from this landing boat to a tractor, we will have to go up to the edge of the reef and unload on the reef. Then we will move across the reef to the beach. The reef is about 450 yards wide. The water, we're told, will be about one or two feet deep. First we may hit boulders or pretty big rocks, then smaller rocks and coral, then mud and underwater grass. There is some danger from potholes and rocks. The halftrack will follow slowly. It is a complex operation. Only a few men will ride in the halftrack—the driver, a radio operator, and a machine gunner. The rest of us will wade—that is, unless conditions are such that we find we can all ride. That decision will be made when we get to the reef.

"There's a sense of anxiousness over this phase of our landing. We don't know how effective our naval and air bombardment will be, and Point Adelup is on our left flank. If they have any big guns there, looking down on us, and they're not knocked out, our halftrack, inching slowly across the reef, will be fair game for potshots. If we get stuck on the reef or our motor stalls in the water, we're that much more of a target for the Jap artillery and mortars. That's why most of us plan to wade at a little distance from the halftrack. None of us knows now what's going to happen. There's lots of uncertainty. As a matter of fact, at any moment the description that's about to follow may end. You'll then know that something has happened.

"Now H-hour is drawing closer. We're still going around and round out here in the water, but we're gradually edging in closer and closer to shore. We've left the transports well to the rear of us now, and we're almost up to the area of the LSTs. They are in a long column with their bows pointed towards shore, and from these bows have come the amphibious tractors that will take in the first assault waves. They should land very shortly. In this tank lighter, the coxswain is still standing without a helmet on—he's behind a shield. However, two other Navy men in here with us are now taking their hoods off their machine guns, getting ready for close-in action.

"There are depth charges being laid out around the transport area. There must be a Jap sub in the vicinity, or perhaps just a warning of one. But we see the explosions in the water. They're well in our rear now—we're not near them. Up above are many flights of American planes. There is a big group of twin-engined bombers and, boy, they look friendly. We are certainly glad that they're ours. And, incidentally, we still have had no opposition in the way of Jap planes or heavy Jap fire—perhaps not peculiar because of the tremendous naval barrage that has been laid down on Guam for so long.

"Now we're passing other landing boats, and men in this boat are waving to men in the other boats they recognize. Some of our men are reading news magazines and other periodicals, trying to keep their minds off what lies just ahead. Some of them are looking at the pages probably without seeing anything. We're so close now that the gunfire around us sounds very heavy. It sounds like a dull, steady rumble, and the entire shoreline shows the effect. There is one big smoke burst after another. Some of them are big fires. You can see orange flames rising hundreds of feet into the air. Now there are flares dropping over some of the sections of the island.

"The assault troops are heading towards the beach now. H-hour will strike at any moment. It's almost eight-thirty in the morning. There's a big fire blazing on the beach. We can see it now. Big, red flames. And there's a battleship to our right, standing in awfully close to shore. They've had no return fire that we can see back to them all morning. Every so often a great orange burst comes from the side of the battleship. There goes one now. And on shore another big smoke column rises. However, there's so much that it's as though the entire shoreline were wrapped in smoke. The smoke is brown in some places, white in others, yellow in others. The bases of the fires are orange and yellow and some even red.

"We're moving in—steadily moving in. There are lots of boats around us. It's funny, it almost seems as if we're at a regatta. It's got a carnival aspect out here, with all these little boats crammed with people, and placards and colored pennants bearing the designations of the various waves, so that they can be easily recognized in case one boat slips away, or so that officers in charge of the control boats can know who's coming up and what beaches they're supposed to land on. It's like a maneuver or a rehearsal. It isn't real. It looks as if everything is blanks, as though nothing is going to come back at us.

"Now there are also American divebombers over the island —plenty of them coming in. We're supposed to have about 900 planes above us—700 to 900, we've been told. Oh! There's a great burst ahead of us now. The men are all leaning forward in this boat anxiously looking ahead. This is all good for us. Makes us feel swell. The water around us is not particularly calm, but it's not rough either—just big swells that don't break over us. When we get to the reef, we hope that we'll be able to wade across calm water.

"Well, our tank lighter is really full. The halftrack looms above us, its 75mm. cannon poking through an armored shield, past the driver's seat. And next to the driver, who's already in place, is the radioman. The armored shields are up all around now. The machine guns—the 50-caliber and the 30-caliber on each side—are loaded and ready. The ammunition boxes are out next to us. We're leaning on one right now. The halftrack is also loaded down with packs and rolls, loose 50-caliber machine guns, tank-destroying bazookas with rocket ammunition, 75mm. ammunition, first-aid kits, five-gallon water cans, rope, carbines, M1 rifles, camouflage netting, and radio transmitters and receivers.

"The little rubber boat that's being towed behind us is for use on the reef for any casualties. If a man is wounded, he will be put on that rubber boat and left there on the reef floating in the water, because other boats will be coming along right away to pick him up. Either they will come from the transports, or else boats that have brought men to the beach will pick up the casualties on the way back. These rubber boats we expect will be floating around there with whoever gets hurt while crossing the reef.

"There is also a unique floating casualty station in operation today. A Navy doctor and eight corpsmen are in one of the landing boats, and they're going to stay at the reef—just about the edge of it—prepared to give emergency treatment, administer sulfa drugs and plasma and emergency dressings, and supervise the transferral of the casualties to the larger boats going back to the transports to evacuate these men. This casualty station will possibly be under fire most of the time, but it's a wonderful way of taking care of anyone who gets hit while crossing the reef.

"The tank destroyer that we're going in with is sometimes called Slapsie Maxie by its men. The crew who are with us include a driver, a gun commander, a gunner, an assistant gunner and loader, two machine gunners, and a radio operator —seven men in all. The trailer behind us holds communications gear as well as flame-throwers. Now all this is going ashore in our boat for immediate use against the beach defenses and anything that lies right behind it. And in our boat, besides the halftrack crew, are other members of this weapons outfit. They include communications men as well as assault troops. I'd like you to meet some of these Marines very briefly. Their attention at the moment is focused on the beach and on the firing going on. Here's one of the machine gunners on the halftrack. He's from Arkansas. How do you feel right now?"

"I feel all right. I never was nervous yet and I'm not nervous now. I'm thinking of Ma and my Dad."

"And here's the gun commander."

"I wish we were up on the beach with the rest of the fellows, but our turn will come soon enough, I guess."

"Here's the communications chief. He hasn't looked nervous all morning."

"I'm not nervous. Just a few butterflies in my stomach."

"Okay. There are a few planes flying over us now—bombers—and we're all looking up. Here's a big, tall, real typical Marine who said he wanted to say something to the folks back home on D-day. Incidentally, this boy is one of our champion gripers. He really believes that's the only right left to a serviceman, and he overworks that right. Now we're going to give him his big chance. Got any gripes to get off publicly just before you go into combat?"

"No. I feel fine. I got the best chow in my pack [C and K rations] and a pair of dungarees."

"Good.—We've just had word that the assault troops have landed and are now on the beach! The LSTs are moving out of range. They're filing off in column, and the tractors that took the first assault troops ashore will come back for the men who are in the small landing boats around us. And very shortly we shall be approaching the reef.—Say [to our radio operator], did you just get a message from the beach?"

"Yeah. I'm listening in to the word from the beach."

"What is it?"

"The landing is successful. The first wave is in."

"Okay! The landing is successful so far on Guam—our first assault wave is on the beach! We're still not ready to go in. That is, this particular wave. But we're still moving closer.

We're getting in there now. The island is assuming definite shape and proportion. We can see perspective.

"And now, here we go! We're streaking in to the line of departure. That means we're going to the line from which we'll shortly leave. The engine of this tank lighter is roaring as we race forward through the water up to a distance of about 2,000 yards from the shore. There's all hell to pay directly ahead of us. The beach looks as though it's on fire. We've just heard word from our radio operator, who's been listening to messages from the shore, that casualties in the first wave were very light. That sounds good. We hope they continue that way as the succeeding waves land. Spray is coming up over us now—and now we're at the line of transfer. We've slowed down. It's just a mass of small boats—small landing craft—LCVPs and LCMs like this one, who have come up, wave after wave, and are waiting now to transfer their men over into the amphibious tractors that will carry them across the reef. The LCMs—the tank lighters—will not transfer their men but will wait here and will go in alongside the men who have transferred into the tractors.

"There's a destroyer right near us. We passed one destroyer camouflaged, standing broadside and firing. And we passed several patrol craft that are controlling the waves going past. There are small control craft bobbing around us here on each side. And again we see that Guam is smoking for a width of about four miles directly in front of us. It's just a mass of smoke. Behind it, through the smoke, you can just see some brown, and then higher up the green hills of the various mountains. The firing you can hear now is coming from battleships and cruisers which are now almost on a direct line with us. They're very close in.

"There are very many American planes diving over the beach and now back of the beachhead—because we are established on the beach. They go into a dive and zoom back up again. There is a float plane, probably an observation plane, above us. We've had no Jap interference from the air. And here are amphibious tractors going past us. Some of them are acting as controls. Others are spares to take over the role of any that get knocked out of action farther in. Most of these little boats now are just bobbing around. They have their different-colored pennants flying in the sun. It's a very bright, hot sun now. They have their placards up so that everybody who's supposed to know will know just what boat is what and where it belongs.

"There is a destroyer coming very close to us now. At least, we're approaching it. You can hear it firing. All hell's being given to the defenders on Guam. There's a terrific racket. One of our boys says: 'Things are hotter here than in Scollay Square in Boston on a Saturday night.' We're trying not to look up too much now. We're beginning to see things splashing in the water. Just a few sudden splashes here and there. They don't look harmful, but you can't tell. The boys have now put on their rifles and carbines again and are getting ready for the moment when we'll hit the reef. There are lots of amphibious tractors—brown ones—bobbing around us—men transferring over. The noise of the boats' engines is blotting out the noise of the shelling.

"Some of the men are beginning to sing here. They're cracking jokes—I guess to hide their nervousness from each other. Now I'm on the deck of the tank lighter, so that I can walk out of this boat as we hit the lip of the reef with the other men—following the halftrack which will be pulling the trailer. We'll be walking behind it and at the sides of it, and some of the men out in front swimming or walking along to keep the halftrack out of any potholes that are in the reef.

"We can hear the stuff whistling now! I don't know whether it's Jap stuff coming near us, or what. The terrific roar around us now is coming mostly from our amphibious tractors. There go American divebombers down on the beach and back of the beach. We can see the beach very clearly now. The coconut trees along the beach are shattered. They look like burned telephone poles. This looks to be a beautiful defensive position in that directly behind the beach are great hills rising up, full of gulleys and draws of all kinds, and we're going to have to storm right up them in the face of the Japs. However, there's been so much naval fire that I don't know what's left there any more.

"Well, we're—we're moving—we're moving in! Still going in. You can see the white sand of the beach very clearly. The roar around us is louder—terrific. The men are sort of watching me for want of something better to do, I guess. Their lips are tight together. However, they're joking on occasion. The water is now a little rough, but we understand that as soon as we get across the reef the surf will be much better. I'll tell you one thing—I don't know how much longer I'm going to want to continue talking, just saying what I'm noticing and thinking. I'm thinking right now of my home and my wife and my little daughter, and I hope they're all right, and I hope I come back to them all right. That's about what you think of now.

"Oh—there's big Jap stuff dropping in the water up ahead of us a little. We'll probably have to go through it. There are great clouds of black smoke. Behind us we can see waves coming after us up to the line of transfer. They're going to follow us in in a few minutes. They're further waves of assault troops. Boy, you can smell the powder in the air now. It's an acrid smell—smoke is all around us. It's getting foggy. It's hard to keep on talking and thinking and trying to figure out for yourself what to do and how to take care of yourself. We'll try, and I hope everything goes off all right. The men are peeking very carefully over the tank lighter, trying to make out what's going on in the water ahead of them. There's a lot of artillery fire around us now—we don't know how much of it is ours. Most of it, I suppose, is coming from our own ships. There's a tremendous destroyer now, even on a line with us, standing just behind the reef, and if they can take it, I guess that we can!

"Now we can see amphibious tanks and regular tanks in ahead of us—they are landing ahead and with us. Here comes an LCI that's been in very close—it's coming out at a fast clip.

"We're slowing down again. The boats around us are slowing down. Maybe we're not going right up to the reef at this moment. One of the NCOs here is telling the men to have their rifles ready and get around the halftrack and act as security for the halftrack as soon as we get ashore. One fellow says now he'd like to go home because he's got his campaign star for this already. However, he's joking. Here comes a fellow with a radio up to the forward part of the boat. The weapons are clicking. The bolts are being pulled back. I've just put the magazine-clip into my own weapon, and we are ready for whatever is going to come.

"Now for the first time we can hear some machine-gun fire on shore. We are very close, but we're not at the reef yet— and then it's more than 400 yards to shore. The reef is near us. We can hear a chattering on shore of machine guns. I don't know how far up the infantry's gotten yet—I doubt whether they've gone very far. There's a terrific clamor coming from shore. And there's a lot of fire and smoke up in the hills now as though our naval bombardment is hitting something. What's that?—Yes, we can see machine guns on the crest now directly ahead of us—firing out at us! Boy, they're coming straight at us now! I want to shift—I think we're a little out of their range. I'm not sure, but I hope so. The fire—you can see—the whole wall is covered with smoke! There's a—I'll explain a little better—there's a cliff at one point—it's that Adelup Point that's on our left—I told you about it—it rises right out of the water. It's been covered with big fire by our own Navy, and the big stuff has been knocked out, but you can see through a wall of smoke a terrific lot of Jap small arms — What's that!—Machine-gun fire, isn't it? It's just a lot of orange dots in the smoke, popping out at us—just haven't been knocked out yet. Somebody's going to have to take it—it will probably be this outfit.

"Well, we're still going in. I imagine we're now well in range of a lot of this stuff. Nothing's hit near us, thank goodness, so far. Here comes a fast speedboat manned by Navy men. They're giving us an order—they're giving our coxswain an order. We don't know what it is—we can't hear it. On the beach we can see lots of American landing boats piled up there, as though they've gone clear up and haven't been able to get off yet. We don't see any figures on the beach yet—we're not that close, or else they're all down flat on their stomachs or have run up past the beach. I don't blame them for not staying there. To our right are a tremendous number of amphibious tractors on the beach. They're piled up there—one is burning! We see an amphibious tractor on fire there—burning. There's a whole long row of them. There's an amphibious tractor going in to our right—another one—

"We're coming up to the reef now! I'm ducking because I don't want to get clipped by anything that's flying high. We haven't passed any burning boats yet. Incidentally, we haven't seen any American planes get shot down—yet. There's a lot of mist around us from the smoke. We can see the amphibious tractors on our right and left filled with Marines—huddled over beneath their big pot helmets—their weapons up on their backs—their machine guns that belong to the tractors pointed up, and the radio aerials waving like fishing rods. Here's one that's a salvage tractor—just waiting here for any tractor that runs into trouble—it will go to its immediate help. And we're coming up near the reef now, I think—and in just a few seconds we're going to run out. I will be about fifteen or twenty feet away from the halftrack, walking through the water. This tank lighter has about six inches of water in it already—

"Here we come up to the reef now! We're going to hold on while we bump! We're going to hit the reef hard so that we catch up on it. And then the coxswain will have to gun the motor as the halftrack goes off—it will have to—it will push the—it will push the—it will push this lighter back.—There! We've hit it! We're grounding on it—we're up on it—we're up on it! In a minute the ramp will go down, and the men will

BACK TO OUR FOXHOLES. *Two men stand guard while a third digs a "community home" among the rocks of northern Iwo.*

JOB DONE. Superfortresses and fighters crowd the newly-wrested first Iwo airfield. Japan now is only 750 miles away.

stream out. A noncom has just wished everyone good luck. A machine gun just fired—our machine gun just fired from this halftrack—three or four shots. The men are now going out ahead—they're moving out ahead of the halftrack. It's very tense at this moment—the men are moving out—Let's go!—Go ahead!—I'm going to follow this halftrack. I can't go ahead of it. The other men are going ahead or at the sides —it's a very tense moment—the men are out on the reef—some of them are wading, some are standing looking around— they're spreading out. We haven't gone over yet. Here we go now—here we go—walking with the halftrack. The halftrack goes down the ramp—into the water—you can hear the splash. —We're now on the reef in the water! I've jumped off—I'm going to wade.

"The water's up to my knees. I think my pistol got wet— I don't know. It's pretty high. I'm moving away from the halftrack now. The men are motioning each other to move forward. The—the surface of the coral is quite level—although it's—it's bumpy. But at least it's not jagged, not full of holes. There's a lot of something growing underneath.

"The halftrack's moving kind of slowly. It's almost a half-mile to the beach. The men are all spread out—they look pretty good. It's a swell picture of these Marines—boys you know from your own home towns. There's a lot of fire around us—but nothing has hit us. Here's some sharp coral sticking up—we're walking over it—you have to be cautious about underwater obstructions. The men are ahead of us and all around us. They're spread out, I should say, about—about a hundred or seventy-five yards in front to about ninety or a hundred yards from side to side. It's—it's quite a job moving your legs through this stuff. You get very tired. You can't go too fast—stumbling—it's pretty rough. I'd say it's about two and a half feet deep. You sort of lose your breath. The boys ahead are stumbling. —Hey! Come on back here! Don't leave me all alone!—There's rifle fire among us now! There are bullets coming through the water! We're—we're trying to zigzag a little. No use—it's machine-gun fire! Gee, one just landed right next to a guy!—What's the matter?—Hey! Spread out! Spread out! Hey!—I'd like to be in the halftrack. Oh, there's a lot of fire coming at us—but no one I can see has been hit—fortunately—amazing. You can't see anything on the beach yet—yes—yes—you can see a Marine running—running through the coconuts. Boy, there's a lot of coral here—just fell over some coral along here.

"You can hear the machine-gun fire coming at us from the Japs in the hills. This is quite—this is quite a moment—the boys are moving along—there's been water up to their necks —some of them have fallen full in and wet everything. And now they're wading by going way down up to their necks— that is to keep themselves underwater. —There's heavy fire falling on us!—We have paused a second—now we go ahead again. Haven't seen any of the men fire yet. Now behind us I can see another halftrack moving through the water and— *whoa!*—our trailer just went over with an awful lot of stuff! Hey—any important gear in that trailer?—The trailer went over—oh, one boy's been hit—one boy's hurt now. They're putting him in the rubber boat—four men are putting him in the rubber boat—I don't know who it is—I can't see him. But he has been hurt, and he's lying on his side—Hold it!— What!—Another boy's hit—another boy's just been hurt! I think he's been killed—our officer is yelling to get him. No, he's all right—he's climbed into the rubber boat—I guess he's all right. There's a lot of fire around us now. We're almost ashore—I'd say about a hundred feet or a little more from shore. There are two Marines now in our rubber boat—What! One of our boys is giving one of those who were hurt a sulfa pill. He doesn't seem too badly hurt—he's on his stomach. And some of the other boys have their mouths drawn and are staring straight ahead—bending down—way down under the water—trying to get their heads—

"There's a tractor backing up past us—there's a boy that's been hurt—right next to us now—he's trying to hang on—

two of them! Hey, Jay—are you all right?—Okay, huh?—
Here's another boy just been hurt—he's hanging onto the
trailer with both arms. Hey, tell them to slow up while they
stick a guy in the trailer!—Oh, there's one Marine lying on his
back on the beach—there's a Marine lying on his back with
blood pouring out of him into the water.

"And here we're reaching the beach now—we're going to
come up on it—and there's fire all around us, and the Marines
are still on the beach! They haven't made any further head-
way—at least, there's a whole—must be two or three waves
here on the beach. In fact, all of the halftracks are lined up
now around us on the beach. None of them have been able to
move up past here. Perhaps farther up there are some Marines
in the hills, but I doubt whether they've gotten there. —
There's very little cover here. There are Marines running
forward around us and men seeking cover—there's one Marine
there—a fellow I know—just been hit in the back of the neck.
His neck is bleeding, but it seems to be a superficial cut.
There's another Marine lying on his back. —The Marines
have been ordered now to disperse and take cover. This is a
very exciting situation. I will say we will get out of it very
easily, but at the moment we don't know how long we'll be
forced to stay here. There's infantry lying around us here. —
There are two—two amphibious tractors piled up next to us.
We are now—now we are huddled down—we're trying to
keep our heads down—we don't know where this fire is
coming from next.

"Marines are going forward one by one. They rise up and
move forward. There are not too many casualties on the
beach, but there are several—sort of sprawled out—well, like
little boys—the corpsmen are walking around—they don't
seem to be taking any cover—they're walking upright looking
for casualties—moving from one guy to the next. Men are
jumping back and forth next to us.

"Now some of the Marines are motioning for the next wave
to come in. And here comes another halftrack behind us with

men coming in after us—they're wading too. We don't think we've left any men in the water. It seems evident that we've been able to take all our casualties out of the water. I don't see any floating. —There's one boy's been pretty badly hurt—lying on his back on the beach with his feet in the water. — One of our own boys has just been shot in the side, but they're taking care of him. It's a little, round black hole—there's some heavy fire now—I don't know what it is—but it's coming at us. Men are being ordered to hit the deck and stay down—and we're just going to wait—we can't move forward because we don't have the beach yet—we're not beyond the beach. There are tanks in here—we do not know what the situation is—you can't tell—there may be Marines well ahead of us, dug into the side of the hill or moving up. It should take us about a day, I imagine, to get to the top of those hills—and here it is only ten minutes of ten.

"Boy!—Something just hit very close—Here's rifle fire too! —I don't see any of the Marines firing—there's nothing in sight to fire at as yet. —Are you okay?—A fellow here has a cramp in his leg. Boy, this is tense. —Here comes another wave coming up. One man just hit the deck—there's plenty of work to do. Boy!—I started to look up and something cracked near, and I went down low again. —I'm sort of running out of breath here—one boy got up, started to run, and fell down again. Don't know whether he got hit—he's lying on his face. Here come more Marines in behind us—they're wading in—fortunately. Seems to me that casualties are light, though every time you see one it makes you feel that there shouldn't be any at all. —And here come more men disembarking at the reef to wade in—Oh!—A shot just hit in the water and missed a man by about six inches. —Here comes a tommy-gunner in —he looks kind of out of breath—his teeth are gritted. He's walking straight toward us standing up—nothing hits him. Finally he just sits down behind us—right behind us and says, 'Oh!'—But he's all right. He's just tired. He's sort of tough-looking.

"Here comes another Marine who kept his rifle dry—Oh, he just fell at the edge of the water, but I think he's still got it dry. He looks around and grins and says, 'Well, what do we do now?'—The amphibious tractors are going right in past us with further waves and seem to be cutting through our own men—at least, going through them. Maybe they're following in to where the infantry is—we hope some of the infantry is in there pretty deep—but there's absolutely no way of knowing. Hey! Don't get up too high—we're trying to shift our position—this is one of those complex personal operations of warfare—it may not seem so important perhaps, but at the moment—

"We're still huddled here—there's no way of knowing what's going on. There's very little you can see at this stage of the battle—even though this is not real jungle warfare. The whole beach is just piled with Marines—they're flat down, hugging the earth, dug in, in foxholes, and huddled behind shattered coconut trees. A few of them will get up every so often and lope forward. It's a very strange thing to watch— one man at a time. There's no concerted action to watch. — One of the men in the halftrack is motioning to us to get away from the halftrack. —Hey, Jay! What's going to happen? Where are you going?—

"They're going to make a dash up the beach. The men who have been hugging the beach behind the halftrack, in the water more or less, are now going to try zigzagging up into the reef—the beach, I mean. I'm sorry—I'm trying to keep conscious of what I'm saying, but it's a little difficult. —The men in the halftrack are going to leave it too—they're going to make a dash for the coconuts—we're all going—we've got to leave the halftrack. —I've got a pistol—we're going up the beach—we're going to dash— . . ."